Name and Subject Index To
The Presidential Chronology Series

Name and Subject Index

Name and Subject Index To

The Presidential Chronology Series

to *The Presidential Chronology Series*

From George Washington to Gerald R. Ford

By
Ronald Gibson

OCEANA PUBLICATIONS, INC.
Dobbs Ferry, New York
1977

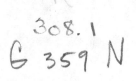

Library of Congress Cataloging in Publication Data

Gibson, Ronald.
    Name and subject index to the Presidential chronology
series.

    (The Presidential chronology series)
    Bibliography: p.
    1. The Presidential chronology series—Indexes.
2. United States—Politics and government—Indexes.
3. Presidents—United States—Biography—Indexes.
I. Title.
Z1236.G5   [E183]   016.973   77-21512
ISBN 0-379-12094-1

Manufactured in the United States of America

An index is a necessary *implement,* and no *impediment,* of a book, except in the same sense wherein the carriages of an army are termed impediments. Without this a large author is but a labyrinth without a clew to direct the reader therein.
THOMAS FULLER, *History of the Worthies of England: Norfolk Writers: Alan of Llyn.*

TABLE OF CONTENTS

INTRODUCTION

The index that follows indicates in capsule form the principal events of American history from the confused, disputatious years leading to Independence along a great arc of time to the day when Gerald Ford bowed out of the presidency.

The long roll of subjects recalls two centuries of American conflict, compromise and achievement. You will find here the almost continuous record of wars and civil wars, of racial smolderings and separateness bursting into clashes and confrontations leading at last to reconciliation if not as yet to a complete comradeship.

You will read of the struggles of labor at first exploited, latterly, at times, exploiting; of financial manipulations; of still-memorized debates and unforgettable assassinations; of perilous treks and explorations only to be followed by the unheeding plunder of man and beast, of land, air and water, followed again in our own time by the resolve to undo this destruction and to restore insofar as we can the beauty and variety of the natural scene.

This full but compact index holds the key to many volumes of presidential history. You will be guided here as to how, and how long, presidents lived and how strenuously they utilized their term of high office for the good of this land and people. Sadly, a number met their death by bullet, their life's work incomplete.

There is much violence in the presidential story, yet there is also an exhilarating thread of aspiration, an ever-scrutinizing dissatisfaction with things as they are out of which discontent we and our 38 presidents have created an abundant, widely shared American civilization.

The Index is comprised of four separate lists:

1. The names of the Presidents in alphabetical order.
2. The name and salient facts about each President arranged in historical order from 1 to 38.
3. A list of all personal names mentioned in both the document and the chronology sections of each volume.
4. An extensive subject list of the matters dealt with in each volume.

In the personal name index and the subject index, the numerals in front of the slash (/) indicate the volume number, that is, the numerical place of the President in the total sequence of 38. The number following the slash indicates the page or pages in the volume. For example, the legend 32 / 26, 35, 40 relates to matters mentioned on pages 26, 35, 40 during the presidency (32d) of Franklin Delano Roosevelt. Subjects and names are arranged in alphabetical order throughout.

LIST OF PRESIDENTS

Numerical

LIST OF PRESIDENTS

1. Washington, George

1732-1789
1789-1797, President

Surveyor, army officer,
politician

1732, Born, Westmoreland
County, Virginia
1775, Commander-in-Chief
1789, Elected first
President of the U.S.A.
1793, Re-elected
1799, Died at Mount
Vernon

2. Adams, John

1735-1826
1797-1801, President

Lawyer, diplomat,
politician

1735, Born, Braintree,
Massachusetts
1785, Ambassador to
England
1789, Vice President
1797, Elected President
1826, Died, Quincy,
Massachusetts

3. Jefferson, Thomas

1743-1826
1801-1809, President

Lawyer, writer,
architect, diplomat,
politician

1743, Born, Albemarle
County, Virginia
1776, Declaration of
Independence
1779, Governor of
Virginia

1785, Minister to France
1790, Secretary of State
1797, Vice President
1800, Elected President
1804, Re-elected
1826, Died at Monticello

4. Madison, James

1751-1836
1809-1817, President

Writer, politician

1751, Born, Port Conway,
Virginia
1779, Member, Continental
Congress
1787, Member,
Constitutional
Convention
1789, U.S. Congressman
1801, Secretary of State
1808. Elected President
1812, Re-elected
1836, Died, Montpelier,
Virginia

5. Monroe, James

1758-1831
1817-1825, President

Army officer, lawyer,
diplomat, politician

1758, Born, Westmoreland
County, Virginia
1776-1778, Fought in War
of Independence
1816, Elected President
1820, Returned unopposed
for second term
1823, Monroe Doctrine
1831, Died, New York City
1858, Re-interred,
Richmond, Virginia

6. Adams, John Quincy

1767-1848
1825-1829, President

Lawyer, diplomat,
  politician

1767, Born, Braintree,
  Massachusetts
1815, Minister to Great
  Britain
1816, Secretary of State
1825, Elected President
1848, Died, Washington,
  D.C.
1848, Interred, Quincy,
  Massachusetts

7. Jackson, Andrew

1767-1845
1829-1837, President

Lawyer, army officer,
  politician

1767, Born, Waxhaw,
  South Carolina
1812, Major General
1821, Governor of Florida
1828, Elected President
1832, Re-elected
1845, Died, Hermitage,
  Nashville, Tennessee

8. Van Buren, Martin

1782-1862
1837-1841, President

Lawyer, politician

1782, Born, Kinderhook,
  New York
1821, U.S. Senator
1829, Secretary of State
1836, Elected President
1862, Died, Kinderhook

9. Harrison, William Henry

1773-1841
1841, President

Army officer, politician

1773, Born, Berkeley
  Hundred, Virginia
1801, Governor, Indiana
  Territory
1812, Major General
1840, Elected President
1841, Died, April 4,
  Washington, D.C. after
  one month in office

10. Tyler, John

1790-1862
1841-1845, President

Lawyer, politician

1790, Born, Charles City
  County, Virginia
1825, Governor of Virginia
1827, U.S. Senator
1841, Vice President,
  March 4
1841, President, April 6
1862, Died, Virginia

11. Polk, James Knox

1795-1849
1845-1849, President

Lawyer, politician

1795, Born, Mecklenburg
  County, North Carolina
1835, Speaker, House of
  Representatives
1839, Governor of
  Tennessee
1844, Elected President
1849, Died, Nashville,
  Tennessee

12. Taylor, Zachary

1784-1850
1849-1850, President

Army officer, politician

1784, Born, Orange
County, Virginia
1824, Superintendent
General, Army
recruiting
1846, General
1848, Elected President
1850, Died, Washington,
D.C.
1850, Re-interred,
Springfield, Kentucky

13. Fillmore, Millard

1800-1874
1850-1852, President

Lawyer, politician

1800, Born, Cayuga
County, New York
1832, U.S. Congressman
1848, Elected Vice
President
1850, President (July)
1874, Died, Buffalo,
New York

14. Pierce, Franklin

1804-1869
1853-1857, President

Lawyer, politician

1804, Born, Hillsborough
County, New Hampshire
1837, U.S. Senator
1847, Brigadier General
1852, Elected President
1869, Died, Concord,
New Hampshire

15. Buchanan, James

1791-1868
1857-1861

Lawyer, diplomat,
politician

1791, Born, Lancaster
County, Pennsylvania
1834, U.S. Senator
1845, Secretary of State
1856, Elected President
1868, Died, Lancaster,
Pennsylvania

16. Lincoln, Abraham

1809-1865
1861-1865, President

Lawyer, politician

1809, Born, Hardin
County, Kentucky
1846, Elected to
Congress
1860, Elected President
1864, Re-elected
1865, Assassinated,
Ford's Theater,
Washington
1865, Buried, Springfield,
Illinois

17. Johnson, Andrew

1808-1875
1865-1869, President

Tailor, army officer,
politician

1808, Born, Raleigh,
North Carolina
1853, Governor of
Tennessee
1857, U.S. Senator
1862, Military Governor,
Tennessee
1865, Vice President
1865, President
1875, Died, Tennessee

18. Grant, Ulysses S.

1822-1885
1869-1877, President

Army officer, politician

1822, Born, Point
  Pleasant, Ohio
1864, Commander of all
  Union armies
1868, Elected President
1872, Re-elected
1885, Died, Mount
  McGregor, New York

19. Hayes, Rutherford B.

1822-1893
1877-1881, President

Lawyer, army officer,
  politician

1822, Born, Delaware,
  Ohio
1865, Major General of
  Volunteers
1868, Governor of Ohio
1877, Elected President
1893, Died, Fremont,
  Ohio

20. Garfield, James Abram

1831-1881
1881, President

Teacher, army officer,
  politician

1831, Born, Cleveland,
  Ohio
1862, Major General
1880, Elected President
1881, Shot, Washington,
D.C., July 2; died,
Elberon, New Jersey,
September 19
1881, Buried, Cleveland,
  Ohio

21. Arthur, Chester A.

1830-1886
1881-1885, President

Lawyer, army officer,
  politician

1830, Born, North
  Fairfield, Vermont
1862, Quartermaster
  General
1881, Vice President
1881, President
1886, Died; buried
  Albany, New York

22. Cleveland, Grover

1837-1908
1885-1889, President

Lawyer, politician

1837, Born, Caldwell,
  New Jersey
1882, Governor, New York
1884, Elected President
1889, End of first
  Presidential term

23. Harrison, Benjamin

1833-1901
1889-1893, President

Lawyer, army officer,
  politician

1833, Born, North Bend,
  Ohio
1865, Brigadier General
1881, U.S. Senator
1888, Elected President
1901, Died, Indianapolis

24. Cleveland, Grover

1837-1908
1893-1897, President

Lawyer, politician

1837, Born, Caldwell,
    New Jersey
1882, Governor, New York
1884, Elected President
1889, End of first
    Presidential term
1892, Elected President
    for a second term
1908, Died, Princeton,
    New Jersey

25. McKinley, William

1843-1901
1897-1901, President

Army officer, lawyer,
    politician

1843, Born, Niles, Ohio
1865, Major
1891, Governor, Ohio
1896, Elected President
1900, Re-elected
1901, Assassinated,
    Buffalo, New York

26. Roosevelt, Theodore

1858-1919
1901-1909, President

Writer, army officer,
    explorer, politician

1858, Born, New York
1895, Police Commissioner,
    New York
1899, Governor, New York
1900, Elected Vice
    President
1901, President,
    September 14
1904, Elected President
    for second term
1919, Died, Oyster Bay,
    New York

27. Taft, William Howard

1857-1930
1909-1913, President

Lawyer, politician

1857, Born, Cincinnati,
    Ohio
1901, Civil Governor,
    Philippines
1904, Secretary of War
1908, Elected President
1921, Chief Justice,
    Supreme Court
1930, Died, Washington,
    D.C.

28. Wilson, Woodrow

1856-1924
1913-1921, President

Writer, university
    president, politician

1856, Born, Staunton,
    Virginia
1911, Governor, New
    Jersey
1912, Elected President
1916, Re-elected
1924, Died, Washington,
    D.C.

29. Harding, Warren

1865-1923
1921-1923, President

Newspaper proprietor,
    politician

1865, Born, Blooming
    Grove, Ohio
1915, U.S. Senator
1920, Elected President
1923, Died, San Francisco,
    buried, Marion, Ohio

30. Coolidge, Calvin

1872-1933
1923-1929, President

Lawyer, politician

1872, Born, Plymouth,
  Vermont
1919, Governor,
  Massachusetts
1921, Vice President
1923, President
1924, Elected President
  for a second term
1933, Died, Northampton,
  Massachusetts; buried,
  Plymouth Notch,
  Vermont

31. Hoover, Herbert

1874-1964
1929-1933, President

Mining engineer, writer,
  politician

1874, Born, West Branch,
  Iowa
1917, Food Administrator,
  World War I
1921, Secretary of
  Commerce
1928, Elected President
1964, Died, New York;
  buried, West Branch,
  Iowa

32. Roosevelt, Franklin D.

1882-1945
1933-1945, President

Lawyer, politician

1882, Born, Hyde Park,
  New York
1921, Contracted
  infantile paralysis
1929, Governor, New York

1932, Elected President
1936, Re-elected
1940, Re-elected
1944, Re-elected
1945, Died, Warm Springs,
  Georgia; buried Hyde Pk.

33. Truman, Harry S.

1884-1972
1945-1953, President

Farmer, army officer,
  haberdasher, politician

1884, Born, Lamar,
  Missouri
1918, Captain, World
  War I
1935, U.S. Senator
1944, Elected Vice
  President
1945, President, April 12
1948, Elected President
  for a second term
1972, Died, Independence,
  Missouri

34. Eisenhower, Dwight D.

1890-1969
1953-1961, President

Army officer, university
  president, politician

1890, Born, Denison,
  Texas
1943, Supreme Commander,
  Allied Expeditionary
  Force
1945, Chief of Staff,
  U.S. Army
1948, President,
  Columbia University
1950, Commander, NATO
  forces
1952, Elected President
1956, Re-elected
1969, Died, Washington,
  D.C.; buried, Abilene,
  Kansas

35. Kennedy, John F.

1917-1963
1961-1963, President

Writer, naval officer,
  politician

1917, Born, Brookline,
  Massachusetts
1943, Lieutenant, U.S.
  Navy
1953, U.S. Senator
1960, Elected President
1963, Assassinated,
  Dallas, Texas; buried,
  Washington, D.C.

36. Johnson, Lyndon B.

1908-1973
1963-1969, President

Teacher, naval officer,
  politician

1908, Born, Stonewall,
  Texas
1949, U.S. Senator
1951, Senate Majority
  Whip
1953, Senate Minority
  Leader
1955, Senate Majority
  Leader
1960, Elected Vice
  President
1963, President (November
  22)
1964, Elected President
  for a second term
1973, Died, Johnson City,
  Texas

37. Nixon, Richard M.

1913-
1969-1974, President

Lawyer, naval officer,
  politician

1913, Born, Yorba Linda,
  California
1951, U.S. Senator
1952, Elected Vice
  President
1956, Re-elected Vice
  President
1968, Elected President
1972, Re-elected
1974, Resigned

38. Ford, Gerald R.

1913-
1974-1977, President

Lawyer, naval officer,
  politician

1913, Born, Omaha,
  Nebraska
1945, Lieutenant
  Commander, U.S. Navy
1948, U.S. Congressman
1965, Minority Leader
1973, Nominated Vice
  President
1974, President (August
  9)

LIST OF PRESIDENTS

Alphabetical

Adams, John, 1735-1826
Second President

Adams, John Quincy, 1767-1848
Sixth President

Arthur, Chester A., 1830-1886
Twenty-first President

Buchanan, James, 1791-1868
Fifteenth President

Cleveland, Grover, 1837-1908
Twenty-second President

Cleveland, Grover, 1837-1908
Twenty-fourth President

Coolidge, Calvin, 1872-1933
Thirtieth President

Eisenhower, Dwight D., 1890-1969
Thirty-fourth President

Fillmore, Millard, 1800-1874
Thirteenth President

Ford, Gerald R., 1913-
Thirty-eighth President

Garfield, James Abram, 1831-1881
Twentieth President

Grant, Ulysses S., 1822-1885
Eighteenth President

Harding, Warren, 1865-1923
Twenty-ninth President

Harrison, Benjamin, 1833-1901
Twenty-third President

Harrison, William H., 1773-1841
Ninth President

Hayes, Rutherford B., 1822-1893
Nineteenth President

Hoover, Herbert, 1874-1964
Thirty-first President

Jackson, Andrew, 1767-1845
Seventh President

Jefferson, Thomas, 1743-1826
Third President

Johnson, Andrew, 1808-1875
Seventeenth President

Johnson, Lyndon B., 1908-1973
Thirty-sixth President

Kennedy, John F., 1917-1963
Thirty-fifth President

Lincoln, Abraham, 1809-1865
Sixteenth President

McKinley, William, 1843-1901
Twenty-fifth President

Madison, James, 1751-1836
Fourth President

Monroe, James, 1758-1831
Fifth President

Nixon, Richard M., 1913-
Thirty-seventh President

Pierce, Franklin, 1804-1869
Fourteenth President

Polk, James Knox, 1795-1849
Eleventh President

Roosevelt, Franklin D., 1882-1945
Thirty-second President

Roosevelt, Theodore, 1858-1919
Twenty-sixth President

Taft, William H., 1857-1930
Twenty-seventh President

Taylor, Zachary, 1784-1850
Twelfth President

Truman, Harry S., 1884-1972
Thirty-third President

Tyler, John, 1790-1862
Tenth President

Van Buren, Martin, 1782-1862
Eighth President

Washington, George, 1732-1799
First President

Wilson, Woodrow, 1856-1924
Twenty-eighth President

PERSONAL NAME INDEX

NAME INDEX

Anne, *Princess*, 37/37
Anthony, Susan B., 21/73
Apgar, Edgar K., 22/3
Appleton, Jane M., 14/2
Appleton, Jesse, 14/2
Appleton, John, 15/19
Aquinaldo, Emilio, 27/8
Arafat, Yasir, 38/22
Arbuthnot, Alexander, 5/16;
  7/7; 10/60
Arias, Harmodio, 32/28
Arista, Mariano, 12/9
Armas, Carlos C., 36/16
Armistad, Walker K., 12/6
Armstrong, Anne, 38/64
Armstrong, John, 4/21,23;
  5/12; 7/5; 9/7
Armstrong, Neil, 37/23
Armstrong, Robert, 7/19
Arnold, Benedict, 1/4,8; 3/9;
  9/1
Arnold, Henry H., 32/79; 34/6
Arnold, Thurman, 32/52
Arthur, Chester A., 19/17,20,
  21,23,25,52; 22/6,7,10;
  23/11; 27/3
Arthur, Ellen, 21/51
Arthur, Ellen H., 21/47,55
Arthur, Malvina S., 21/45
Arthur, William, 21/45,52
Arthur, William L.H., 21/48,50
Ash, Roy L., 37/59; 38/24
Ashburton, *Lord*, 8/19; 10/67;
  15/7
Atchinson, David R., 12/16
Attlee, Clement, 31/32; 33/14,
  15,16,20,38
Aury, Louis, 5/14
Austin, Harmon, 20/3,7
Austin, Warren, 33/7
Avery, Sewell, 32/94
Axson, Ellen L., 28/2,3,12

B

Babcock, George, 13/62
Babcock, James F., 16/12
Babcock, Orville E., 18/7,13,
  14
Bache, Benjamin F., 2/11,14;
  3/24,25
Bacon, Robert, 26/19; 27/12
Badger, George, 9/14
Baez, Buenaventura, 18/7
Bagot, Charles, 5/14,15
Bailar, Banjamin, 38/30,70
Bainbridge, William, 4/21

Baker, Bobby, 36/32,35
Baker, E.D., 16/5
Baker, Edward, 16/18
Baker, James A., 38/89
Baker, Newton D., 26/24,25;
  28/16
Baker, Ray S., 28/24
Balaquer, Joachin, 36/46
Baldwin, Robert, 11/11
Ball, George W., 35/7; 36/34,
  66
Ball, Joseph, 33/9
Ballinger, Richard A., 27/15,
  16,17,20
Bancroft, George, 8/15; 11/8,
  10,11,12,16; 12/7
Bankhead, William B., 32/51,65;
  36/4
Banks, Nathaniel, 16/21,22,27,
  30
Banning, Henry B., 19/8
Barbe-Marbois, Francois de,
  3/35
Barber, Anthony, 37/50
Barbour, James, 6/11,14
Barbour, Philip B., 8/18
Barcelo, Carlos R., 38/103
Barclay, Hugh, 2/17
Barclay, Robert H., 9/7
Barghoorn, Frederick, 35/18
Barker, Bernard, 37/77
Barker, Wharton, 20/27; 23/12
Barkley, Alben W., 32/90;
  33/29; 36/10
Barnes, William, Jr., 26/21,24
Barry, Edward P., 30/5
Barry, John, 2/11
Barry, William T., 7/13
Barton, Bruce, 30/22; 32/65
Baruch, Bernard, 32/50,82;
  33/20
Bass, Lyman K., 22/2
Bates, Edward, 16/14,38
Batista, Fulgencio, 34/33;
  36/25
Baxter, Elisha, 18/12,13
Bayard, James, 4/22; 6/7
Bayard, Thomas F., 20/27;
  21/59,78; 22/6; 24/20,25
Beame, Abraham, 38/16,38,39,
  53,56,72
Beauregard, P.G.T., 16/16
Beckley, John, 3/27
Belcher, Mrs., 2/1
Belknap, William W., 18/7,12,
  14,15; 20/23
Bell, David, 35/7,14
Bell, John, 9/14; 10/74; 11/4;
  16/12
Bendit, Daniel C., 36/61

Benedict, E.C., 24/21
Bennett, Floyd, 30/21
Bennett, Henry G., 33/37
Bennett, Hugh H., 32/39
Benson, Ezra T., 34/14
Benton, Jesse, 7/5,13
Benton, M.E., 22/10
Benton, Thomas H., 7/5,13,18,24;
  8/12; 10/64; 12/18,21
Berkeley, Norborne, 3/3
Berle, Adolph A., 32/18,52;
  35/7,10
Berlin, Irving, 34/8
Berhard, *Prince*, 38/77,89
Berrien, John, 7/12,13
Berrigan, Rev. Philip F., 37/43
Beveridge, Albert J., 23/16;
  25/15; 26/21; 27/19
Bevin, Ernest, 31/32
Bibb, Mortimer, 11/10
Biddle, Francis, 32/70,93;
  33/13
Biddle, Nicholas, 5/22; 7/45,
  74; 8/9; 13/53
Bingham, Robert, 32/23,51
Binh, Nguyen T., 36/67
Binns, John, 7/10
Birchard, Sardis, 19/1,2,8
Birney, James G., 8/17; 11/9
Bishop, Robert H., 23/1
Bissell, *Governor*, 16/10
Bissell, Wilson S., 22/3,18;
  24/20,26
Black, Eli, 38/35
Black Hawk, 7/14
Black, Eugene R., 32/37
Black, Hugo L., 32/49; 36/11;
  37/48
Black, Jeremiah S., 15/11,16
Black, Shirley T., 37/47
Blackmun, Harry A., 37/34,35
Blaine, Alice, 21/67
Blaine, James G., 18/14; 19/9,
  10,15,17; 20/20,22,27,28,29,
  30,31; 21/60,67,71,75,77;
  22/4,5; 23/10,12,13,15,16,17,
  18,21,22,23; 25/6; 26/4; 27/3
Blaine, Walker, 23/19
Blair, Francis B., 7/12,14,18
Blair, Francis P., 20/17
Blair, Francis P., Jr., 16/18;
  17/27
Blair, Montgomery, 16/15,37
Blakeley, William, 36/29
Bland, Richard, 19/18
Bland, Richard P., 20/25
Blatchford, Samuel, 21/62
Bliss, Cornelius N., 25/9

Bliss, Ray C., 34/67
Bliss, *General* Tasker, 28/23
Bliss, William S., 12/7,15,24
Blodgett, Eleanor, 32/1
Bloom, Sol, 32/96
Bloomer, Elizabeth, 38/2
Blount, James H., 24/20,22
Blount, William, 7/2
Blount, Winton M., 37/15,43
Boettiger, Anna, 32/90
Boggs, Hale, 37/44,53,57
Boggs, Henry, 18/3
Bok, Edward, 32/11
Boland, William P., 33/2
Boldt, George H., 37/49
Bolivar, Simon, 9/10; 29/7
Bonaparte, Charles J., 26/15,17
Bonaparte, Napoleon, 2/16,17;
  3/27,29,33,34,35,39,41; 4/11,
  12; 6/7
Boorstin, Daniel, 38/52
Booth, John W., 16/42
Borah, William E., 28/25;
  29/5,8; 32/57
Borden, William L., 34/18
Borie, Adolph E., 18/6,7
Bork, Robert, 37/70
Borman, Frank, 36/68; 38/101,
  103
Bosch, Juan, 36/31,41,46
Botts, John M., 10/69
Bouck, William, 30/15
Boutwell, George S., 18/6,12;
  20/18
Bouvier, Jacqueline, 35/5
Bowers, Claude G., 32/23
Bowles, Chester, 32/88; 33/18,
  21; 35/7,15
Boyd, Alan S., 36/49
Boynton, *General* H.V., 19/11,12
Braddock, Edward, 1/2
Bradford, William, 1/17
Bradley, Joseph, 20/24
Bradley, Joseph P., 18/8,9;
  19/13
Bradley, Omar, 33/33,36
Brady, John R., 21/59
Brady, Matthew B., 16/31
Brady, Matthew C., 11/21
Brady, T.W., 20/32
Bragg, Braxton, 16/24,25,28,29;
  17/9; 18/4
Bragg, Edmund S., 22/18
Bragg, Walter L., 22/11
Branch, *Judge*, 13/58
Branch, John, 7/11,12,13
Brandegee, Frank B., 29/5
Brandeis, Louis D., 27/17,26,
  29; 28/16; 32/48

French, Stephen B., 21/52
Freneau, Philip, 1/13,15,16;
  3/14,18
Frick, Henry C., 22/19; 23/23;
  26/13,18; 27/18
Fries, John, 2/15
Fromentin, Elijius, 5/19
Fromme, Lynette A., 38/49,55,
  59
Frost, Robert, 35/18
Fry, Thomas, 3/1
Fukuda, Takeo, 38/102
Fulbright, J.W., 33/39; 36/19,
  45,56,57
Fuller, Melville W., 22/13;
  23/17; 24/20; 27/14,19
Fulton, Robert, 3/41
Furness, Betty, 37/19

G

Gadsden, James, 14/9
Gaffney, Jack, 22/3
Gagarin, Yuri, 35/9
Gage, Lyman, 25/8; 26/9
Gage, Thomas, 2/4
Gallatin, Albert, 2/12; 3/24,
  33,34; 4/17,22; 5/16; 6/7,
  13; 8/6
Galloway, Samuel, 16/11
Galt, Edith B., 28/15
Gandhi, Indira, 36/45; 38/41,
  42,43,105
Gandhi, Mohandas K., 31/32;
  32/81
Gardiner, Alexander, 10/72
Gardiner, David, 10/69
Gardiner, Henry D., 21/47,50
Gardiner, Julia, 10/69,70
Gardner, John W., 36/42
Gardoqui, Don Diego de, 5/3
Garfield, Abram. 20/1
Garfield, Eliza B., 20/1
Garfield, Harry A., 20/10;
  28/20
Garfield, James, 19/10,11,14,
  23,24,25; 26/17
Garfield, James A., 18/16;
  23/9,10,11
Garfield, Lucretia, 20/3
Garland, Augustus H., 22/6
Garner, John N., 31/23,24;
  32/17,19,44; 33/7,31; 36/3
Garretson, Joseph, 24/32
Garrison, Lindley M., 28/9,15
Garrison, Lloyd, 32/36
Gary, Elbert, 26/18

Gates, Horatio, 1/6
Gates, Thomas, 37/32; 38/74
Gay, James A., 25/8
Gazley, William, 9/9
Geary, John W., 14/12; 15/11
Genet, *Citizen*, 6/3
Genet, Edmond C., 1/15,16,17;
  3/16,17,18
Genovese, Eugene D., 37/12
George, *King of Greece*, 32/80
George III, *King*, 2/2,8,9;
  3/37,40,41
George VI, *King*, 32/53
George, Henry, 26/4
George, Walter F., 32/53;
  36/15
Gerard, James, 32/6
Geronimo, 22/7
Gerry, Elbridge, 2/11,14;
  3/24,44; 4/21,23
Gesell, Gerhard A., 37/71
Giancana, Sam, 38/42
Gibbons, Sam, 38/29
Gibson, Andrew, 38/21
Gibson, Hugh S., 30/22
Gidding, Joshua, 12/14
Gilbert, Prentiss B., 31/19
Gildersleeve, Virginia, 32/96
Giles, William B., 1/14,15;
  2/12; 3/15,16,20,23; 10/59,
  65
Gillhaus, August, 29/4
Gilman, Daniel G., 24/28
Gilmore, Gary, 38/104
Gilpin, Henry D., 8/17
Giraud, Henri, 32/86
Gitlow, Benjamin, 30/16
Glass, Carter G., 28/23;
  31/22
Glavis, Louis R., 27/16,17
Glenn, John, 35/11; 36/29
Glover, John, 1/4
Godkin, E.L., 21/50,76
Goethals, George W., 26/18;
  27/12
Goff, Nathan, Jr., 19/25
Goldberg, Arthur J., 35/7,13;
  36/42,60
Goldwater, Barry M., 34/65, 66;
  36/36,38; 37/11,12,78; 38/5,
  69,83
Gompers, Samuel, 22/10; 26/3;
  27/17; 30/6
Gumulka, Vladimir, 36/58
Goodell, Charles E., 37/25,39,
  41; 38/4-7,11,16,31,34
Goodhue, Andrew, 30/9
Goodwin, Richard, 35/7,8
Gore, Albert A., 37/41

Johnson, Herschel, 15/15;
  16/12; 20/4
Johnson, Hiram W., 28/8,25;
  29/5; 30/7
Johnson, Hugh S., 32/27,37
Johnson, Jacob, 17/1
Johnson, James, 17/16-18
Johnson, Joshua, 6/4
Johnson, Louis, 32/63,81;
  33/32,36; 36/13
Johnson, Louisa C., 2/11
Johnson, Lucy B., 36/9,46,52
Johnson, Lynda B., 36/7,54,67
Johnson, Lyndon B., 31/39;
  33/30,47,48,49; 34/57,65-69;
  35/6,19; 37/8,9,11,12,13,15,
  38,61,66; 38/4,5,6
Johnson, Martha, 17/2
Johnson, Mary, 17/2,29
Johnson, Mary M., 17/1
Johnson, Rebecca B., 36/1,29
Johnson, Reverdy, 12/17
Johnson, Richard M., 8/11,17;
  9/8,11,13; 10/65,66
Johnson, Robert, 17/2,28
Johnson, Roy W., 34/40
Johnson, Sam E.,Jr., 36/1,5
Johnson, Smith, 8/8
Johnson, William, 3/37
Johnston, Albert S., 16/20;
  18/4
Johnston, Joseph E., 16/22,34,
  40; 17/15
Johnston, Sarah B., 16/1
Jones, Jacob, 4/21
Jones, James C., 11/6
Jones, James K., 24/27
Jones, Jesse, 32/24,31,64,86,
  95
Jones, John P., 21/59
Jones, Joseph, 5/1
Jones, Thomas, 10/68
Jones, Thomas G., 26/9
Jones, William, 4/21,22
Jonkman, Bartel, 38/2
Joseph, *Chief*, 19/16,17
Joy, James F., 20/28
Juan Carlos, 38/56,80
Judd, Walter H., 34/67
Julian, George W., 13/63,
  14/7
Jumonville, Sieur do, 1/2
Jupiter, 3/27
Justo, Agustin, 32/46

K

Kadama, Yoshio, 38/77
Kahn, Ayub, 36/54
Kalb, Johann de, 1/6
Kalinin, Mikhail, 32/58
Kalmbach, Herbert W., 37/55,
  56,77; 38/26
Kane, Elisha K., 14/8
Katsura, *Count* Taro, 27/11
Katzenbach, Nicholas, 36/40
Kearney, Stephen W., 11/14,16
Kefauver, Estes, 33/41; 34/32;
  35/5; 36/12,19,20,21
Kelley, Clarence M., 37/66;
  38/44,77,85,88,90,95
Kellogg, Frank B., 27/16;
  30/15,18,19,23,25,27; 31/13,
  14,16,19
Kellogg, William P., 18/13
Kelly, John, 21/55,77
Kendall, Amos, 7/18,45; 8/13,
  17
Kendrick, Anna, 14/1
Kendrick, John B., 29/11;
  30/8
Kennedy, Caroline B., 35/5
Kennedy, David M., 37/15,42
Kennedy, Edward M., 35/1,13;
  37/23; 38/17,27,74
Kennedy, Jacqueline, 35/5,10,
  11,12,14
Kennedy, John F., 31/37,38;
  32/36; 33/47; 34/57,58,60,61,
  62,63,64; 36/18,20,21,22,24,
  25-33,38; 37/8,9,11,66; 38/4,
  59,101
Kennedy, John F.,Jr., 35/6
Kennedy, Joseph, Jr., 35/3
Kennedy, Joseph P., 32/36,51,
  68; 35/1
Kennedy, Patrick B., 35/17
Kennedy, Robert F., 34/70;
  35/1,5,7; 36/25,33,38,49,58,
  61,62; 37/13,14,19
Kennedy, Rose F., 35/1
Kennedy, T.B., 30/19
Kern, John W., 26/19
Kernan, Francis, 21/55
Kerner, Otto, 36/53
Kerr, Robert, 36/12
Key, David M., 19/15,17,19,23
Key, Francis S., 4/23; 5/12
Keynes, John M., 32/30,34,52
Keyserling, Leon H., 33/21
Khrushchev, Nikita, 34/31,41,
  49,51,53,55,56,57,59; 35/9,

Mansfield, Mike, 36/21,29;
37/43,53; 38/35
Manson, Charles, 37/38
Mao Tse-tung, 36/46; 37/52;
38/12,55,60,90,95
Marburg, Theodore, 27/26
Marbury, William, 2/17
Marcantonio, Vito, 37/4
Marcos, Ferdinand, 36/47;
38/100
Marcy, William, 11/10; 12/8,
10; 13/53
Marcy, William L., 8/3,20;
14/8
Mardian, Robert, 37/74; 38/26
Marland, Sidney P.,Jr., 37/39
Marsh, Joseph, 2/1
Marshall, George C., 32/56,74,
79,84; 33/10,17-19,23,25,32,
36,46; 34/4,5,6
Marshall, Humphrey, 20/6
Marshall, James W., 18/13
Marshall, John, 2/11,16,17;
3/31,32,40,41; 4/14,15,26,
27; 5/1,4,13,17,19,24; 7/14,
17; 8/13
Marshall, John R., 26/23
Marshall, Thomas R., 28/8
Marshall, Thurgood, 36/43,52
Martin, Graham, 38/31
Martin, Joseph, 38/3
Martin, Joseph W., 32/65;
33/39
Martin, *Rev.* Thomas, 4/1
Martin, William M., 36/50
Martin, William M.,Jr., 37/26,
31
Martine, James E., 28/7
Martinez, Eugenio R., 37/77
Martling, Abraham, 8/1
Marvin, William, 17/17,19
Mason, George, 3/8,10
Mason, James, 14/10
Mason, James M., 16/18
Mason, John Y., 11/10,16;
15/10
Masten, Arthur, 21/81
Mateos, Lopez, 34/47,65
Matthews, F.D., 38/42,58
Matthews, Stanley, 19/4,11,
13,14,25,26; 20/24
Maurer, James H., 31/22
Maury, *Rev.* James, 3/2
Maverick, Maury, 36/4,14
Max of Baden, *Prince*, 28/22
Maxwell, Russell L., 32/63
Maynard, Horace, 19/23
Mazzei, Philip, 3/22,23
Mead, James, 33/9
Meade, George G., 16/26,27

Meany, George, 37/53; 38/13,15,
46
Medary, Samuel, 11/8
Meigs, Jonathan, Jr., 4/22;
5/14
Meigs, Jonathan R., 8/5
Meigs, Montgomery C., 16/18
Meiklejohn, Alexander, 30/10
Meir, Golda, 37/39
Mellon, Andrew W., 29/7;
30/10,11,18; 31/21
Mercer, Lucy, 32/7
Meredith, James, 35/13; 36/46
Meredith, William M., 12/17
Merriam, C.H., 26/2
Merritt, Edwin A., 19/18,20,
21,52; 21/54
Merritt, Wesley, 25/12
Merry, Anthony, 4/12
Meskill, Thomas, 38/36
Metcalf, Victor, 26/13,17,19
Meyer, George von L., 26/17;
27/15,18
Michaelis, *Lt.Col.* J.H., 34/9
Mifflin, Thomas, 1/18
Miki, Takeo, 38/46
Milanowski, John P., 38/2
Miller, Charles E., 21/81
Miller, Samuel F., 16/23
Miller, Tom, 36/5,20
Miller, William E., 34/65;
36/36,38; 37/11
Miller, William H.H., 23/8,17
Milligan, Jacob L., 33/6
Milligan, L.P., 20/15
Milligan, Maurice, 33/8
Mills, Roger Q., 22/13
Mills, Wilbur D., 36/43,53
Minckwitz, *Dr.*, 26/1
Minot, Henry, 26/2
Minow, Newton N., 35/7
Minthorn, Henry J., 31/1,2
Minton, Sherman, 34/33
Miranda, Francisco, 4/13
Mitchell, James P., 34/17
Mitchell, John, 24/31
Mitchell, John N., 37/12,15,
52,55,56,65,66,67,74,75;
38/26,95,101
Mitchell, Martha, 37/55
Mitchell, O.M., 20/7
Mitchell, William B., 30/20
Mize, Robert, 33/2
Moffet, James A., 32/36,41
Moley, Raymond, 32/18,22,27,28
Molotov, Vyacheslav, 32/63,80,
94,95,97; 33/12,25; 34/20
Moncada, *General*, 30/24
Mondale, Walter, 38/59,85,95
Mondell, Frank W., 30/15

Monroe, Eliza K., 5/4,10
Monroe, Elizabeth J., 5/1
Monroe, James, 1/17,21; 2/12,
    18; 3/9,20,24,31,35,36,40,42,
    44,45; 4/5,7,11,12,14,15,17,
    20,21,23,24,25,27; 6/7-10;
    7/7,8; 8/4,5; 9/8; 20/4
Monroe, James, Mrs., 5/4,24
Monroe, Maria H., 5/8,18
Monroe, Spence, 5/1
Montgomery, John B., 11/15
Montgomery, Richard, 1/4
Moody, William H., 26/10,11,
    13,17; 27/12,19
Moore, Frederick, W., 27/4
Moore, Sara J., 38/51,61
Moore, Thomas P., 9/10
Moorer, Thomas H., 37/34
Morgan, Arthur E., 32/25
Morgan, Edward L., 37/17,18,81
Morgan, Edwin D., 21/47,48,49,
    53,60,67
Morgan, Ernest, 38/44
Morgan, Harcourt, 32/25
Morgan, J.P., 21/50; 24/26,28;
    26/10,13,18; 27/18; 32/23
Morgan, *General* John, 19/5
Morgan, William, 8/8
Morganstierne, *Ambassador*, 34/8
Morgenthau, Henry, Jr., 32/14,
    22,29,30,94
Morgenthau, Robert, 33/14
Morrill, Lot M., 18/15
Morris, Gouverneur, 1/15,17;
    5/5
Morris, Gouverneur, II, 3/31
Morris, Newbold, 33/41
Morris, Robert, 1/9; 2/16;
    9/2
Morrissey, Patrick, 22/3
Morrison, Ralph W., 32/25
Morrison, William R., 22/11
Morrow, Dwight, 30/20,25,26,
    30,31
Morse, Charles W., 27/22
Morse, Edward S., 32/3
Morse, Samuel F.B., 16/36
Morse, Wayne, 35/6; 36/13,15,
    18
Morton, Julius S., 24/20
Morton, Levi P., 20/29,31;
    21/56; 22/13; 23/15,24,25
Morton, Oliver P., 19/9,15;
    23/4,5,9,12
Morton, Paul, 26/13
Morton, Rogers, 37/42,43,59;
    38/20,22,51,57,60,64,73,89
Morton, Thurston, 36/53
Moses, Bernard, 27/7,8
Moses, Robert, 32/12,13

Moskowitz, Belle, 32/13
Motley, John L., 18/6,9
Mott, Lucretia, 11/19
Mott, Martin, V., 6/14
Moyers, Bill D., 35/8
Moynihan, Daniel P., 37/27,42;
    38/36,48,53,57,59,60,61,66
Mueller, Frederick H., 34/50
Muhlenburg, Frederick A., 1/9,
    21
Mundt, Karl, 37/3
Munsey, Frank A., 27/24
Murchison, Charles, 22/14
Murphy, Charles F., 32/7
Murphy, Frank, 32/55,59
Murray, Mrs., 19/1
Murray, Philip, 33/42
Murray, William V., 2/15,16;
    3/26,27
Murrow, Edward R., 35/7;
    36/34
Muskie, Edmund, 34/71; 36/65,
    66,67; 37/14,51,52,53; 38/55
Mussolini, Benito, 32/45,53,
    56,57,86
Myers, Frank S., 27/29

                    N

Nagako, *Empress*, 37/48
Nagel, Charles, 27/15
Napoleon, *see* Bonaparte
Napoleon, Louis, 17/12,19
Nation, Carry, 27/14
Nations, Gilbert O., 30/15
Neagle, David, 23/18
Nedzi, L., 38/41
Nehru, Jawaharlal, 32/81;
    34/39
Nelson, Donald M., 32/62,72,
    78,93
Nelson, John, 11/10
Nessen, Ron, 38/22,54,55,62
New, Harry S., 29/14; 30/10,
    11,18
Newberry, Truman H., 26/19;
    29/8,10
Newett, George, 26/23
Newman, *Rev.* J.P., 18/17
Newton, Isaac, 16/22
Nhu, Ngo D., 35/18
Nicholas, I., 15/5
Nicholas, Wilson C., 3/44,45
Nicholls, Francis P., 19/14,
    15,16,19
Nickerson, Ansell, 2/3
Niles, John M., 8/17
Nimitz, Chester W., 32/77,91;

Potter, Clarkson N., 19/19-21
Pound, T.L., 20/27,28
Powell, Elihu N., 16/9
Powell, Lewis F.,Jr., 37/49,
  50; 38/86
Powers, Francis G., 36/27
Prajadhipok, *King*, 31/18
Pratt, Fanny A.H., 19/3
Pratt, William A., 19/1
Preston, Thomas, 2/3
Preston, William B., 12/17
Price, Byron, 32/77
Priestly, *Dr.* Joseph, 3/27
Prince, L.B., 19/18; 21/54
Procter, William, 28/6
Proctor, Henry A., 9/7
Proctor, Redfield, 23/18
Prophet, *The*, 9/4-6
Proxmire, William, 37/11;
  38/47,81
Pujo, Ansere, 28/9
Pulaski, Casimir, 1/7
Putnam, James, 2/1

Q

Quay, Matthew S., 23/16
Quesada, Elwood R., 34/45
Quezon, Manuel, 32/42
Quincy, Josiah, 2/3,4

R

Rabin, Yitzhak, 38/102
Raborn, William F., 36/41
Ramsey, Alexander, 19/22,24,25
Randall, Charles H., 30/15
Randall, Clarence B., 34/17
Randolph, Edmund, 1/11,16,17,
  19,20; 3/5,19,20; 5/6,7; 6/3
Randolph, James M., 3/38
Randolph, John, 5/9,10; 6/13;
  10/62
Randolph, Payton, 3/5,6
Randolph, Robert B., 7/15
Randolph, Thomas M., 3/1,13
Randolph, Thomas M.,Jr., 3/13,
  36
Randolph, Thomas M. Jr., Mrs.,
  3/13,37,38
Randolph, William, 3/1
Rankin, Jeanette, 28/18
Raskob, John J., 32/15
Rawlins, John A., 18/6,7
Ray, Dixy L., 38/42

Ray, James E., 36/59
Rayburn, Sam, 32/65; 33/47;
  36/3,5,9,14,19,20,25,27,29
Raymond, Henry J., 16/36
Reagan, Ronald, 34/68; 37/13,
  14; 38/32,51,58,60,61,63,64,
  67-70,72-78,80-82,84,85,87,
  88,92,96,104
Rebozo, Charles G., 37/13,24
Record, George L., 28/6
Redfield, William C., 28/9
Reed, Stanley F., 32/51;
  34/38
Reed, Thomas B., 23/19,20;
  24/22; 25/5,7,8
Reeder, Andrew H., 14/9,11
Regan, Frank S., 31/23
Rehnquist, William H., 37/49,
  50
Reid, John, 7/6,7
Reid, John C., 19/10
Reid, Whitelaw, 20/29; 22/18;
  23/22,23
Reinhardt, Fraulein, 32/1
Remini, Robert V., 8/8
Renick, Edward J., 28/1
Reuss, Henry, 38/49
Revere, James W., 11/15
Reynolds, James, 5/5
Reynolds, Verne L., 30/14
Rhea, John, 5/15,24
Rhodes, James, 38/60
Rhodes, John, 37/78
Ribicoff, Abraham, 35/7
Richardson, Elliot L., 37/35,
  59,65,66,70; 38/9,10,24,46,
  49,56,61,94
Richardson, Joseph, 6/17
Richardson, William A., 18/12
Richberg, Donald R., 32/37
Richey, Charles R., 37/80;
  38/28
Ridgeway, *General* Matthew B.,
  33/39; 34/12
Riensberg, Miss, 32/1
Riis, Jacob, 26/5
Riley, Bennett, 12/17
Riley, James W., 23/28
Rines, William C., 8/10
Rives, John C., 7/18
Rives, William C., 10/66
Robards, Lewis, 7/3
Robb, Charles, 36/54
Robb, Lucinda, 36/67
Roberts, Owen J., 31/15; 32/48
Roberts, *Col.* William H., 19/10
Robertson, Donald, 4/1
Robertson, William H., 20/32,
  33; 21/58

S

Work, Hubert,   29/11,14,15;
   30/10,18,28
Worth, William J.,   11/16
Wright, Fielding L.,   33/29
Wright, Luke E.,   26/19; 27/7,8
Wright, Silas,   8/8,14,20;
   11/7,8
Wyman, Louis,   38/50
Wynne, Robert J.,   26/13
Wythe, George,   3/2,8,9

X

XYZ,   2/11,12

Y

Yarborough, Ralph,   36/22
Yates, Eugene A.,   34/21
Yates, Richard,   16/8; 18/3
York, Sarah,   7/13
Yost, Charles W.,   37/42
Young, Brigham,   12/10; 15/12
Young, David,   37/47,69
Young, John,   36/40
Young, Owen D.,   30/12; 31/13
Young, Sol,   33/1
Young, Thomas L.,   27/3
Youngs, William,   26/8
Yrujo, *Marquis* de Casa,   4/11,
   12,13

Z

Zahir, *King* Mohammed,   34/64
Zahn, *Rev.* John,   26/23
Zangara, Giuseppe,   32/21
Zarb, Frank,   38/22
Zetterberg, Stephen,   37/4
Zhukov, *Marshal* Gregory V.,
   34/7
Ziegler, Ronald L.,   37/10,14,
   64,66
Zumwalt, Elmo,   38/60
Zwicker, Ralph,   36/17

SUBJECT INDEX

SUBJECT INDEX

A

ABOLITION
  Boston mob violence, 13/82,
    84
  petition in D. C., 15/6

ADMINISTRATION OF JUSTICE See
  Justice

AERONAUTICS
  Bureau of Civil Aviation,
    31/9
  capacity, aircraft industry,
    33/119
  civil aviation security,
    37/39
  Commerce Dept., inspection,
    30/108
  first plane flown, 26/12
  Lindbergh's flight to Paris,
    30/25
  SEE ALSO Hijacking

Agency for International Development, 35/10,48

AGRICULTURE
  Agricultural Adjustment Acts
    parity prices under, 32/25,
      51
  Cotton Control Act, 32/33
  Department created,16/21;22/15
  Farm Credit Administration,
    32/23, 26
  farmers' aid, 32/47
    acts listed, 30/90
  Federal Crop Insurance Cor-
    poration, 32/51
  Federal Farm Board, 31/13
  McNary-Haugen Bill
    subsidized exports, 30/100
    vetoes, 30/103, 119
  moratorium on foreclosures,
    32/35
  price supports program,
    37/42
  re-vitalization, 32/109
  Soil Bank Bill, 34/31
  surplus grain to India, 34/55

AIR FORCE ACADEMY established,
  34/19

ALABAMA (STATE)
  re-admitted, 17/27
  seceded, 15/17

ALABAMA
  sunk by *Kearsage*, 16/34

ALABAMA Case
  Geneva Tribunal, 18/10, 63
  Joint High Commission, 18/9
  President's comments, 18/57
    63
  Treaty of Washington, 18/9,
    10, 63

ALASKA
  acquisition, 17/60
  entered Union, 34/43, 46
  indigenous land titles,
    37/50
  settlement, 26/12
  statehood proposed, 33/86
  treaty for purchase, 17/24
  SEE ALSO New States

ALIEN ACT See Alien and Sedition Acts

ALIEN AND SEDITION ACTS, 2/47,
  51, 53, 55
  SEE ALSO Kentucky and Virginia
    Resolutions; Naturaliza-
    tion

ALIEN ENEMIES ACT See Alien
  and Sedition Acts

ALIENS
  deportation, 2/51, 53
    of ex-Communists, 34/21
  facilities for displaced
    persons, 33/75
  Japanese relocated, 32/78
  Mixed Claims Commission,
    report, 30/115
  registration, 29/107
  scrutiny, 32/63
  SEE ALSO Alien and Sedition
    Acts; Kentucky and Virginia
    Resolutions

ALLIANCE FOR PROGRESS, 35/8,
  48, 67

BULWER CLAYTON TREATY, 12/21

BUREAU OF CIVIL AVIATION
established, 31/9

BUREAU OF CORPORATIONS See
Department of Commerce

BUREAU OF REFUGEES See
Freedmen's Bureau

BURLINGAME TREATY
attempted violation, 21/91
Chinese immigration, 19/21

BURR'S PLOT
Jefferson's refusal to obey
subpoena, 3/98
proclamation, 3/94, 96

BUSINESS PRACTICES
anti-trust measures, 26/41,
51
corporate accounts, pub-
licity, 26/68
Elkins Act, 26/17
government supervision,
26/31
Interstate Commerce Act,
26/31
SEE ALSO Interstate Com-
merce; Interstate Commerce
Act; Interstate Commerce
Commission
investigations, tobacco
and sugar trusts, 26/86
name, use of, 26/89
political contributions,
26/78; 37/52, 67
race discrimination, private
contractors, 36/29
railroad investigation,
26/17
railroad rates, 26/32
Standard Oil
Elkins Act violations,
26/17
secret rates, 26/16
stockholders' lists, 26/89
supervision, 26/89
Bureau of Corporations,
26/51
of trusts, 26/33
SEE ALSO Trusts and Monopolies

BUSING
Detroit, opposed, 37/55
Nixon's opposition, 37/52
warning on over-use, 37/48

C

CABLE ACT, 29/12

CALIFORNIA
admitted to Union, 13/59
annexation, 11/15
cession, 11/65
Compromise of 1850, 12/28
free state controversy, 12/20
statehood supported, 12/28
SEE ALSO Mexico

CALIFORNIA, UPPER
acquired, 11/77

CAMBODIA
invasion, 37/34, 35, 36,
67, 122

CANADA
civil war, 8/65
Reciprocity Treaty
fishing rights, 14/9
tonnage duties, 21/138

CARNEGIE PEACE FOUNDATION
created, 27/19

CARNEGIE STEEL WORKS
Homestead clash, 22/19

CAROLINAS
re-admitted, 17/27

CARPETBAG GOVERNMENT, FLORIDA,
19/12

CASABLANCA CONFERENCE, 32/84

CENSUS
1840, 10/98
fact-gathering agency, 20/18
ten-yearly, 1/11

CENTRAL AMERICA
British relations, 14/56, 71
private territorial aggres-
sions, 14/53

CENTRAL INTELLIGENCE AGENCY
  anti-Castro plot, 35/8
  training Cuban exiles, 35/6

CHARLESTON, S. C.
  arsenal seized, 15/17

CHEROKEE INDIANS See Indian
  Tribes (American)

CHEYENNE INDIANS See Indian
  Tribes (American)

CHICKAMAUGA BATTLEGROUND
  as national park, 24/27

CHICKASAW INDIANS See Indian
  Tribes (American)

CHILD LABOR
  constitutional amendment
    recommended, 29/108
  Keating-Owen Act, 28/17
  prohibition, 31/7; 32/53

CHILE
  civil war, 23/67

CHINA
  commercial relations, 14/26
  Communist take-over, 33/34
  exterritoriality, 26/39
  invaded Assam, India, 36/31
  invitation to Nixon, 37/138
  Kissinger's secret visit,
    37/47
  Nixon's visit, 37/52, 160,
    161
  railroad loans, 27/47
  territorial integrity,
    31/20, 83
  treaties, recognition,
    10/134
  treaty limiting immigrants,
    19/24
  Treaty of Amity, 15/13
  United States-China agree-
    ment on Taiwan, 37/161
  SEE ALSO Boxer Rebellion

CHINESE EXCLUSION ACT, 21/63;
  22/14
  vetoed, 21/91

CHINESE IMMIGRATION
  upheld, 21/62
  SEE ALSO Burlingame Treaty

CHIPPEWA INDIANS See Indian
  Tribes (American)

CHOCTAW INDIANS See Indian
  Tribes (American)

CHURCH AND STATE
  Mormon polygamy question,
    15/38; 20/40
  separation, 3/56; 4/17, 59

CIRCUIT COURT OF APPEALS
  created, 23/21

CITIZENSHIP
  Puerto Rican nationals,
    28/19
  SEE ALSO Naturalization

CIVIL DEFENSE
  shelter program, 35/46

CIVIL RIGHTS
  Alabama National Guard
    mobilized, 35/16
  Alabama University federal
    orders, 35/79
  Civil Rights Act, 36/36,85
  Civil Rights Bill of 1866,
    17/20, 48
  Commission on equal job
    opportunity, recommended,
    34/133
  Committee on Civil Rights
    created, 33/74
  court decision on anti-war
    protests, 37/45
  credit agencies, 37/41
  extended by amendments,
    36/138
  Federal Bureau of Investiga-
    tion, powers extended,
    34/131
  Fifteenth Amendment, 18/8,
    31
  immigrants, 18/10
  interstate transport, 34/28
  Little Rock, school desegre-
    gation, 34/38, 115
  Louisiana elections, 18/82
  march on Washington, 35/17;
    36/32
  mass demonstrations, Bir-
    mingham, 36/31
  Montgomery bus boycott, 34/29
  Negroes, 18/13
  obstruction of court orders,
    34/131

CIVIL RIGHTS (Continued)
Panama Canal Zone, 33/93
power to inspect election
records, 34/132
power to investigate denied
rights, 34/37
public places, 36/36
racial segregation in
schools, 34/20
referendum refused, 34/36
removal of inequities recom-
mended, 33/91
school integration, Supreme
Court ruling, 37/30
Selma confrontation, 36/40
Southern Manifesto, 36/19
students' rights, 37/101
voting irregularities,
34/56
Voting Rights Bill, 36/105
voting supervision, 34/50
women, 18/66
SEE ALSO Amnesty Act; Ku Klux
Klan; Naturalization

CIVIL SERVICE
English system, 21/89
federal, 21/66
merit system introduced,
19/16, 17
political activities for-
bidden, 32/57
reform, 19/31, 35, 77, 80;
21/85, 103; 24/78
SEE ALSO Pendleton Act
staff classification, 30/84
tenure, 20/40
SEE ALSO Civil Service Commission; Spoils System

CIVIL SERVICE COMMISSION
civil service reform, 22/77
first report, 21/130
rules, 21/69
scrutiny, 19/72

CIVIL WAR
begins, 14/15
fall of Richmond, 16/41
Fort Sumter fired on,
10/75; 16/15
Gettysburg address, 16/126
Kansas outbreak, 15/10
Peninsular campaign, 16/22
recruitment, 23/32
save the Union, paramount
object, 16/23
Shenandoah campaign, 19/5

CIVIL WAR (Continued)
Sheridan's ride, 16/37
surrender at Appomattox
Court House (Lee), 16/41
SEE ALSO *Alabama* case;
Amnesty Act; Battles

CIVIL WORKS ADMINISTRATION,
32/29

CIVILIAN CONSERVATION CORPS,
32/23

CLAIMS, PERSONAL
Monroe's request, 5/75

CLAYTON ANTI-TRUST ACT See
Trusts and Monopolies

CLAYTON-BULWER TREATY, 15/30

COAL
national ownership, 26 /97
profiteering, public safe-
guards, 30/43

COASTAL DEFENSE, 3/100

COEUR D'ALENE
silver miners, violence,
23/23

COINAGE ACT, 18/11
decimal system, 1/14

COLD WAR
Communist aggression, 34/80
Hungarian revolt suppressed,
34/33
Russia, mutual reconnais-
sance offer by U. S.,
34/134
Russian invasion of Czechoslovakia, 36/65
U-2 incident, 34/55, 56,
58, 134
SEE ALSO Berlin; Foreign Relations

COLOMBIA
Panamanian 'revolt', 26/12
transit guarantees, 19/82

COLORADO
admitted to Union, 18/15
territory formed, 15/18

COLUMBUS SPEECH See Slavery

COMMAND OF THE ARMY ACT, 20/16

COMMERCIAL RECIPROCITY,
    TREATIES, 21/134

COMMISSION ON CAMPUS UNREST,
    37/36, 39

COMMISSION ON EQUAL JOB OPPOR-
    TUNITY
    recommended, 34/133

COMMITTEE ON CIVIL RIGHTS,
    33/74

COMMITTEE TO RE-ELECT PRESIDENT
    "dirty tricks", 37/48

COMMUNICATIONS
    Federal Communications Com-
        mission, 32/35
    national planning, 32/110
    Russo-U. S. hot line, 35/16
    SEE ALSO Radio; Television

COMMUNISM
    Middle East warning, 34/100
    Truman's attack on, 33/101

COMPROMISE OF 1850, 13/69, 87

CONFEDERATE STATES OF AMERICA
    formed,1861, 20/4
    pardon, 17/27, 28

CONFERENCE OF NATIONS
    First, 1899, 26/73

CONFLICT OF INTEREST
    public officers, 22/51

CONGO
    U. S. support for U. N.,
        35/30

CONGRESS
    first bill, 1/10
    Southern restoration ob-
        structed, 17/58
    SEE ALSO Impeachment

CONGRESS OF INDUSTRIAL ORGAN-
    IZATIONS
    formed, 32/42

CONSCIENTIOUS OBJECTORS See
    Military Draft

CONSERVATION
    Alaskan fisheries, 30/41
    Bering Sea seals, 27/5
    bird reservation, 26/12
    Civilian Conservation Corps,
        32/23
    Columbia River, U.S.-Canada,
        36/34
    flood control, 30/28
    forests, 26/20, 35
    Grand Canyon game preserve,
        26/16
    Highway Beautification Act,
        36/44
    inventory of natural resour-
        ces, 26/19
    jet port banned, Everglades,
        37/30
    laws passed, 36/64
    Lincoln's opinion, 16/98
    national forest reserves,
        26/20
    Newlands Conservation Act,
        26/10
    oil spills, laws, 30/41
    President Johnson's achieve-
        ment, 36/138
    public grasslands, 32/36
    reckless use of resources,
        26/95
    soil, 26/95; 32/39
    Soil Conservation Act, 32/39
    timber, 26/95; 29/108
    water supply, 26/35
    waters, Great Lakes, 27/29
    waterways development, 26/92
    wildlife, 26/48
    Wilson's inaugural appeal,
        28/33

CONSPIRACY
    alleged, Lincoln's death,
        17/33

CONSTITUTION
    Agricultural Adjustment Act
        unconstitutional, 32/42
    Amendments See Amendments
    budget question, 27/78
    checks and balances, 4/6
    cloture vote in Senate,
        36/11
    Cooper Union speech, 16/90
    direct presidential voting
        advocated, 17/61
    Madison as father role,
        4/6

CUBA (Continued)
Civil War, 25/28
clashes with Spain, 14/26
destitute Americans in,
25/27
diplomatic relations sev-
ered, 34/61
evacuation, 26/46
exports, 18/102
future relations with U.S.,
25/68
independence, 25/13
intervention, 17/61
mediation, 18/7
military requested, 25/47
naval blockade lifted, 35/14
rebels, 18/8, 34
revolt, 24/26
Russian alliance announced,
36/25
Russian missile bases, 35/13
Russian troops leave, 35/15
Russo-U. S. confrontation,
35/53
strategic importance, 15/43
strife, 18/11, 65, 93
ultimatum, 25/47
United States aid ended,
34/56
United States base, Guan-
tanamo, 34/52
United States warning to
Great Britain and France,
13/61
warning to aggressors, 14/54
SEE ALSO *Black Warrior*; Central Intelligence Agency;
Maine; Ostend Manifesto;
Platt Amendment; Spain;
Spanish American War;
Treaties: Paris, 1898

CUMBERLAND ROAD, 5/56

CURRENCY
Coinage Act, 18/11
gold reserve, 24/106
gold/silver question, 20/39
Legal Tender Act, 18/8, 9
paper money opposed, 4/6
redemption in coin, 20/39

CZECHOSLOVAKIA
Russian invasion, 36/65

D

DAKOTA TERRITORY FORMED, 15/18

DAWES ACT, 22/8

DAWES PLAN
German reparations, 30/12,
14, 16

DEBTORS, POWER OF, 2/25

DECLARATION OF INDEPENDENCE,
3/8, 49

DEFENSE
Adams on need for increased
army and taxes, 2/31, 39
Armed Forces strength,
33/119
Australia-New Zealand
security pact (ANZUS),
33/40, 43
Department proposed, 33/63
Eisenhower letter to Bul-
ganin, 34/119
guided missiles to Great
Britain, 34/35
Kennedy's assessment, 35/46
mission to France to secure
support for, 2/38
nuclear test-ban treaty,
35/17
occupation of Germany ended,
34/26
SEATO established, 34/23
strategy reappraised, 35/31
troops in Thailand, 35/12
United States-Nationalist
China Pact, 34/23
waste exposed, 33/10
SEE ALSO Army; Navy

DELAWARE INDIANS See Indian
Tribes (American)

DENMARK
Virgin Islands, 17/25, 60

DEPARTMENT OF COMMERCE
Bureau of Corporations,
26/51, 60

DEPARTMENT OF STATE
created, 1/10

DEPARTMENT OF WAR
created, 1/10

DEPORTATION, 2/51, 53; 34/21

DEPRESSIONS
1893-1897, 25/22
hunger marches, 31/20
SEE ALSO Financial Panics;
One Hundred Days

DETENTE
Helsinki Conference, 38/141
nuclear weapons, U.S.-Russia,
36/121
United States-Russian Agreement, 37/66

DETROIT
surrender to British, 5/12

DISARMAMENT
Armed Forces reduced, 29/43
Geneva Conference, 34/97
germ warfare stocks des-
troyed, 37/28
manpower cuts, 37/218
naval, 29/65
United States policy since
1920's, 35/77
Vladivostock Agreement,38/169
Washington Arms Conference,
28/28
Four-Power Pact, 29/10, 85

DISASTERS
Idaho dam, 38/80
Johnstown flood, 23/50
Kentucky coal mine, 38/71
Mississippi floods, 30/112;
31/10

DISCRIMINATION
Armed Forces, 33/30; 34/88
federal employment, 33/30
federal housing, 35/14
federal government, 34/88
private contractors to
government, 36/29

DISPLACED PERSONS See Aliens;
Refugees

DOMINICAN REPUBLIC
messages to Congress (Grant),
18/69, 71
treaty to annex, 18/7,32,49
rejected, 18/8
United States intervention,
17/61; 36/99
United States marines in,
36/41, 42, 46

DRAFT See Military Draft

DRED SCOTT CASE
decision, 15/11; 16/10
'house divided' speech,
16/56
SEE ALSO Lincoln-Douglas
Debates

DRUGS
hazardous, control of,35/18
milder penalties, 37/41
opium import banned, 22/11
untested, 35/13

DUMBARTON OAKS
Planning Conference, 32/92

E

EDUCATION
aid to poor schools, 36/41
campus unrest, Commission
on, 37/36, 39
college costs, 35/44
Department of Health, Education and Welfare
created, 34/15, 92
Elementary and Secondary
Education Bill, 36/98
four-year program, 34/39
head start, pre-school program, 36/102
Higher Education Facilities
Act, 36/75
Negro children, 16/21
scholarships for poor students, 36/44
school segregation, 37/26
Little Rock, 34/115
students' rights, 37/101
teacher qualifications,35/29

EEL RIVER INDIANS See Indian
Tribes (American)

EGYPT
Anglo-French-Israeli forces
invade, 34/33
United States opposes in-
vasion, 34/33

EL DORADO
Spanish attack on mail
steamer, 15/32

ELECTIONS
campaign spending, 37/40,
41, 52

ELECTIONS (Continued)
    Electoral Commission crea-
        ted, 19/13
    enforcement of laws, 19/49
    military interference,
        19/61
    Nixon vs. Helen Gahagan
        Douglas, 37/4
    Portugal, first in 50 years,
        38/75

ELECTORAL COLLEGE
    abolition proposed, 11/2;
        17/27
    Act passed over veto, 17/54
    popular vote compared,
        23/16
    reform, 21/78

ELKINS ACT, 26/17

ELLSBERG CASE, 37/51, 65
    "covert operation", 37/47
    Ehrlichman's part, 37/69,78
    Pentagon Papers, 37/46
    "plumbers'" burglary, 37/48
    SEE ALSO Watergate

EMANCIPATION PROCLAMATION
    arguments against, 16/117
    condemned by Pierce, 14/15
    draft, 16/23
    issued, 16/25
    Lincoln on Fremont, 16/113
    "stump speech" letter,
        16/122
    text, 16/120

EMBARGO ACT, 3/102
    repealed, 3/102

EMBARGO BILL
    1812 war, 4/96

EMERGENCY BANKING RELIEF ACT,
    32/22

EMPLOYERS' LIABILITY See
    Labor Laws

ENERGY
    Alaskan oil pipeline, 37/72
    Boulder Dam project, 30/29,
        114; 31/12
    coal, inadequate management,
        30/81

ENERGY (Continued)
    Columbia River, United
        States-Canada agreement,
        34/59, 61
    Energy Policy Office, 37/67
    Federal Energy Administra-
        tion, 37/75
    Muscle Shoals, 30/46, 51,
        80
    Niagara Falls power plant,
        34/37
    President rebukes Congress,
        38/138
    Public Works Bill, 31/18
    Tennessee Valley Authority
        empowered to sell revenue
        bonds, 34/49

ENVIRONMENT
    Clean Air Bill, 37/43
    Florida canal halted, 37/43
    pesticide control, 37/58
    thirty-seven-point program,
        37/130
    urban decay, 37/119
    water Quality Improvement
        Act, 37/33
    SEE ALSO Conservation; Pollu-
        tion; Reclamation; Waters;
        Waterways

EPISCOPAL CHURCH BILL, 4/59

ERSKINE AGREEMENT
    trade agreement, 4/39

ESKIMOS
    Alaska, land titles, 37/50

ESPIONAGE, 34/17, 22, 38
    Central Intelligence Agency
        Chile, 37/79; 38/15
        mail opened by, 38/32, 51,
        86
    Coplon and Gubichev, 33/32
    death penalty, 34/22
    domestic spying, 37/66
    Federal Bureau of Investiga-
        tion burglary, 38/72
    Frederick Barghoorn released,
        35/18
    prosecution expedited, 34/20
    report on Central Intelligence
        Agency, 38/40
    Rosenbergs executed, 33/39
    World War 1, 28/20
    SEE ALSO Central Intelligence
        Agency, Civil Rights;
        Watergate

FINANCE (Continued)
   money changers indicted,
     32/108, 109
   securities, full disclosure,
     32/26
   Security and Exchange Com-
     mission created, 32/34
   stock exchange deals, regu-
     lation, 32/31, 34

FINANCIAL INQUIRIES
   New York, 38/145
   Prince Bernhard, 38/77, 89

FINANCIAL PANICS
   bank failures, 31/77, 97
   "Black Friday", 18/7
   Black Thursday, 1929, 31/14
   gold investigation, 20/19,
     21
   'Great Panic', 1893, 24/21
   March 1933, 32/117, 118
   National Cordage Co., 24/21
   New York Stock Exchange,
     1857, 15/12
   1907, 26/17, 18
   stock market crash, 30/30;
     31/14

FIRESIDE CHATS
   banking explained, 32/117
   "court packing" plan, 32/139
   early actions explained,
     32/121
   financial crisis explained,
     32/117
   inflation control, 32/187
   one hundred days, recovery
     measures explained, 32/128
   Pearl Harbor, history of
     Fascist oppression, 32/170
   radio, first, 32/22

FISCAL CORPORATION BILL
   veto, 10/67, 91

FISHING RIGHTS
   clash with Britain, 14/26,
     80

FIVE NATIONS OF INDIANS See
   Indian Tribes (American)

FLAG
   established, 5/15
   new 50 star flag, 1960,
     34/57

FLORIDA
   Jackson's campaign, 5/34
   land annexed, 4/17
   re-admitted, 17/27
   seceded, 15/17
   warning to foreign powers,
     4/58

FLORIDA, WEST
   annexation, 4/48, 52

FOOD
   administration, World War 1,
     31/4
   rationing, World War 1,
     31/4
   SEE ALSO Health

FORCE BILL
   Negro voting rights, 23/20

FORD'S THEATRE, 16/42

FOREIGN AID
   Agency for International
     Development, 35/10, 48
   Alliance for Progress
     established, 35/8, 48, 67
   America's contribution,
     33/75
   Belgian relief, 31/4
   Biafra, Nigerian civil war,
     36/64
   birth control excluded,
     34/52
   European Recovery Program,
     33/27, 28
   food for Europe, 31/5
   food for India, 36/45
   Food for Peace Program,
     35/48
   Foreign Assistance Act,
     free nations, 36/33
   French relief, 31/4
   Kissinger stipulates condi-
     tions, 38/63
   Korea, Republic of, 34/94
   reduced, 37/21, 141
   routed through U N agencies,
     33/107
   to Congo, 35/13
   South Vietnam, 34/24
   two categories: knowledge
     and goods, 33/106
   underdeveloped lands, 33/105
   SEE ALSO Alliance for Progress;
   Marshall Plan

GOLD
California, 11/79
production, effect on
prices, 13/92
convertibility suspended,
37/142
Gold Standard Act, 25/15
off gold standard, 32/24
panic investigation, Gar-
field's report, 20/19
Public Credit Act, 18/6;
20/18
reduction of reserves,
25/19
run on gold, threat to
dollar, 36/57

GOOD NEIGHBOR POLICY, 32/110

GRAND ARMY OF THE REPUBLIC
See Republican Party

GREAT BRITAIN
ALABAMA case See *ALABAMA*
Case
British ships banned, 3/41
Extradition Treaty rejected,
22/15
first ambassador to, 24/20
Hudson's Bay claims, 16/32
indemnities, War of 1812,
6/14
Jay Treaty, 4/9
minister to, 5/25
Northwest Boundary, 18/11,
64, 100
Oregon agreement, 6/15
St. Lawrence River, 18/47
Treaty of Amity, 2/41
Treaty of Commerce, 21/71
United States declares war,
6/6
Venezuela boundary dispute,
24/111
SEE ALSO American Samoa;
World War 2.

GREAT LAKES
declared high seas, 24/23
naval forces limited, 5/36

GREAT SOCIETY
Johnson's program announced,
36/39, 89

GREECE See Truman Doctrine

GUADALUPE-HIDALGO TREATY,
11/18, 19, 73; 15/8

GUAM
acquired, 25/14
ceded, 25/13

GUN CONTROL
crime statistics, 36/132
easy purchase condemned,
36/133
presidential efforts,
36/132; 38/159
shotguns and rifles, no
effective control, 36/133

GUN-FOUNDRY BOARD
appointed, 21/68

H

HABEAS CORPUS
limited, 16/28
suspended in Kentucky,
16/35
suspended in South Carolina,
18/10, 54, 56

HAITI
recognized, 16/22
return of Negroes, 16/30
United States troops withdrawn, 32/36

HAMPTON ROADS PEACE CONFERENCE,
16/39

HARPER'S FERRY
Buchanan's opinion, 15/50
John Brown's Raid, 14/14
Lincoln's opinion, 16/99

HARRISON LAND LAW See Land

HAWAII
admitted to Union, 34/47, 50
annexed, 23/72; 24/30;
25/55
commercial treaty, 18/13
king's visit, 18/13
protectorate, 23/20
ended, 24/21
reciprocity treaty, 21/125
Republic proclaimed, 24/24
revolution, 23/20; 24/88
statehood proposed, 33/86

HAY-BUNAU VARILLA TREATY,
26/12

HAY-HERRAN CONVENTION
land lease, Isthmus of
Panama, 26/11
rejected by Colombia, 26/12

HEALTH
ban on DDT, 37/28
cancer research, 37/50
care impeded by unclear
laws, 34/89
child labor, 26/59; 29/108
Keating/Owen Act, 28/17
prohibited, 31/7; 32/53
citation to Jonas Salk,
polio vaccine, 34/96
Clean Air Bill, 37/43
communicable diseases
eradication, 35/44
contested drugs, 35/13
day-care centers, 37/50
Department of Health,
Education and Welfare
created, 34/15, 92
disability benefits, coal
miners, 37/29
Federal Narcotics Control
Board established, 29/11
federal-state program for
the aging, 34/50, 58
food
additives, precaution,
34/44
adulterated, 26/77
Food, Drug and Cosmetic
Act, 32/53
Meat Inspection Act,
26/16
Pure Food and Drug Act,
26/16
sanitation, 28/34
germ warfare stocks destroy-
ed, 37/28
Great Society proposals,
36/39
half holidays, 26/81
hazardous drugs control,
35/18
insurance advocated, 26/21
mass immunization program,
35/43
Medicare, 36/103
bill signed, 36/43
mothers, D. C., 30/84
Narcotics Prohibition Act,
26/19

HEALTH (Continued)
national health survey,
34/31
Negroes, shorter life expec-
tancy, 35/80
Occupational Health and
Safety Act, 37/43
poverty no bar to care,
37/131
pre-paid medical insurance,
33/99
rail workers, excessive
hours, 26/72
school physical tests,
31/7
Sheppard-Towner Act
child and maternity wel-
fare, 29/10
smoke nuisance, 26/77
working women, 26/59

HEALTH, EDUCATION AND WELFARE
DEPARTMENT
created, 34/15, 92

HIGHWAYS
Highway Trust Fund
use for mass transit, 37/68
interstate highway development, 34/25, 31
post-war program, 32/94
road to Pacific, 14/33

HIJACKING See Terrorism

HIROSHIMA, 33/55
SEE ALSO World War 2

HOMESTEAD
bill vetoed, 15/15, 56;
17/4
violence, steel industry,
23/23

HONDURAS
British encroachment,
14/57, 73

HOOVER COMMISSIONS
re-organizations under,
31/33, 35

HOOVER DAM
formerly Boulder Dam, 31/33
SEE ALSO Energy

HOT LINE
Arab-Israeli war, 1967,
36/124

I

INDIAN TRIBES (Continued)
Kickapoo
  ceded land, 9/5
Miamie
  ceded land, 9/3
  land title extinguished,
    8/76
Nez Perce
  war, 19/16, 17
Ottawa
  removal, 8/74
Pawnee
  Reservation enlarged,21/64
Piankeshaw
  ceded land, 9/4
Potawatomie
  ceded land, 9/4
  removal, 8/74
  treaty, 16/20
Pottawatomie Creek
  massacre, 14/12
Sac, 3/105
  ceded land, 9/4
  land title extinguished,
    8/76
  treaty, 16/20
Seminole
  continued resistance,
    8/77, 106
  land, 21/136
  removed to Oklahoma,21/72
  war, 5/14, 15
Seneca
  treaty, 1/62
Shawnee
  treaty, 16/32
Shoshone
  land disposal, 21/61
  treaties, 16/30
Sioux
  ceded land, 13/103
  land title extinguished,
    8/76
  treaties, 13/103
Ute
  conflict, 22/12
Weas
  ceded land, 9/5
Winnebagoe
  land title extinguished,
    8/75
Wyandotte
  treaty, 1/30
SEE ALSO Battles; Indians
  (American); Treaties

INDIAN WARS (AMERICAN) See
  Battles

INDIANA (TERRITORY), 9/3

INDIANS (AMERICAN)
  emancipation, 22/8, 37
  federal aid, 32/24
  foreign interference, 2/41
  full citizenship, 30/15
  Indian Affairs Superinten-
    dent, 5/20
  Indian Bureau investigations,
    19/16
  Indian Removal Act, 7/23
  Indian Reorganization Act,
    32/35
  Interior Department report,
    30/114
  lands, penalties, unlawful
    entry, 21/67, 76
  peace treaty, 1815, 9/8
  protection, need for, 24/78
  reformed management, 18/47
  removal west, 7/36, 101,108
  reservations, 18/22, 65
  tax exempt lands, 32/44
  title to Alaska lands, 37/50
  title to New Mexico lands,
    37/42
  treatment of, 18/70, 73, 99
  use by British, 4/80
  SEE ALSO Indian Territory;
    Indian Tribes (American)

INDUSTRIAL LEGISLATION See
  Labor Laws

INDUSTRY
  loan to Lockheed, 37/47
  National Industrial Recovery
    Act, 32/26
  National Recovery Adminis-
    tion Codes, 32/27

INFLATION
  acts vetoed, 18/11, 74
  fixed income group, 32/195
  SEE ALSO World War 2.

INTERIOR DEPARTMENT
  created, 11/21; 12/16

INTERNAL SECURITY ACT
  passed over veto, 33/36

INTERNATIONAL AID
  UNRRA established, 32/88

INTERNATIONAL AMERICAN BANK
  advocated, 23/54

LABOR LAWS (Continued)
women and children, 32/44

LABOR VIOLENCE
Boston Police strike,
30/6
coal mines, Arkansas,
30/68
coal mines, Colorado,
28/10,11
Homestead, 23/23
mine strikebreakers, 29/11
Molly Maguires hanged,
19/16
railroad battles, 19/17
Republic Steel, 32/49
Roosevelt's warning, 26/57
silver miners, Coeur
d'Alene, 23/23
strikers fired on, 24/24
suppression of gangsterism,
34/45
widespread arrests, 28/26

L'AMISTAD
slave cargo freed, 8/16

LAND
Harrison's Land Law, 9/3

LATIN AMERICA
aid policy promised, 28/41
closer commercial ties,
28/41
no territorial aims, 28/41
Organization of American
States, 33/28
SEE ALSO Alliance for
Progress; Monroe Doctrine

LEAGUE OF NATIONS
Covenant presented, 28/101
defeated in Senate, 27/28;
28/26
Harding's opposition, 29/6,
17
Hoover's support, 31/5
Roosevelt's views, 26/25
Wilson's campaign, 28/25

LEBANON
civil war begins, 38/35
marines in, 34/43

LECOMPTON CONSTITUTION See
Kansas

LEGAL TENDER ACT, 18/8,9

LEND-LEASE
agreement with Russia,
32/80
ended, 1945, 33/15
SEE ALSO World War 2

LIBERIA
established, 5/23
order restored, 27/47
recognized, 16/22

LIBERTY LOAN ACT, 28/20

LIBRARY OF CONGRESS
burned by British, 4/23
established, 2/16

LINCOLN-DOUGLAS DEBATES,
16/10,11,62

LOGAN ACT, 2/15

LONDON NAVAL TREATY, 31/15

LOUISIANA
Constitution, 16/131
election dispute, 18/13,81
Federal troops in, 18/13,
82
re-admitted, 17/27
seceded, 15/17

LOUISIANA PURCHASE, 3/36,74,
80,82

LOUISIANA STATE LOTTERY, 23/62

LUSITANIA
Notes to Germany, 28/14
sinking of, 26/24; 28/14

M

MAIL DELIVERY FRAUDS, 20/32

MAINE
blown up, Havana, 25/30
destruction, 25/44, 45

MANCHURIA
Japanese invasion, 31/19

MANHATTAN PROJECT, 32/82

MANILA CAPTURED, 23/27

"MARCH TO THE SEA"
General Sherman, 16/38

MARINES
defense of Wake Island,
  32/183
end of Nicaraguan occupa-
  tion, 31/27
Haiti evacuated, 32/36
in Dominican Republic,
  34/67; 36/41, 42, 46
in Lebanon, 34/43
in Nicaragua, 30/21
John Brown seized, 20/3
Marine Corps established,
  2/14

MARITIME COMMISSION
created, 32/44
load lines, vessels,
  safety, 30/41

MARSHALL PLAN, 33/25

MARTIAL LAW
Chicago, 24/24, 105
Kentucky, 16/35
Pullman strike, 24/105

MAYAGUEZ
Cambodia seizes U. S. merchant ship, 38/38

MAYSVILLE ROAD BILL
veto, 7/29

MEDAL OF HONOR
created, 16/23

MERCHANT MARINE
expansion, 32/67, 181
government aid, 29/99;
  30/28
need to maintain, 30/33
return to private enter-
  prise, 30/129
revival, 18/8, 29; 25/24
United States Maritime Commission created, 32/44
United States Merchant
  Marine Academy, 34/30
vessels armed, 32/75
War Shipping Administration,
  32/78
SEE ALSO Maritime Commission

MERIT SYSTEM See Civil Service

MEXICAN WAR, 10/71, 114;
  11/14, 55, 63
Mexico City falls, 11/17
peace treaty, 11/18, 19
President's message, 11/49
SEE ALSO Guadalupe-Hidalgo
  Treaty

MEXICO
boundary, 14/12, 27, 43
  clashes, 18/64, 100
California dispute, 11/10
ceded California, 15/8
ceded New Mexico, 15/8
Claims Commission, 18/71,
  101
Extradition Treaty, 16/22
recognized, 5/20
severed relations, 11/10
Texas dispute, 11/37
war with United States,
  15/8

MIAMI INDIANS See Indian
Tribes (American)

MIDDLE EAST
Arab boycott of Israel,
  38/31
Arab-Israel war, 1967,
  36/52
blockade, Gulf of Aqaba,
  36/51
disengagement of forces,
  37/214
Palestine Liberation Or-
  ganization (PLO), 38/19
United Nations troops
  withdrawn, 36/51
warning to Communists,
  34/100

MIDNIGHT APPOINTMENTS, 2/17

MIDWAY ISLAND
possessed, 17/25

MILITARY DRAFT
age reduced to 18, 32/83
Civil War, 16/27, 28, 31,
  32, 33, 35, 39
compulsory peacetime training, 32/58
conscientious objectors,
  Supreme Court ruling,
  37/36
Conscription Bill, 1940,
  32/63

MILITARY DRAFT (Continued)
    deferments ended, 37/34
    extended, 32/70, 71; 37/48
        Selective Service Act,
        33/120
    Korean War, 33/35, 39
    lottery, 32/65; 37/28
    peacetime draft extended,
        34/47
    Proclamation, May 1917,
        28/86
    Pueblo incident, 36/55
    registration, 32/64
    reserve and national guard,
        35/46
    riots, New York, 16/27
    Selective Service Act ex-
        tended, 35/15
    service extended, 32/72
    SEE ALSO Recruitment

MILITARY-INDUSTRIAL COMPLEX
    Eisenhower's warning, 34/143

MILITARY OCCUPATION
    Japan, 1945-1951, 33/15

MILITARY RULE
    in South, 17/23, 24
    SEE ALSO Reconstruction

MILITIA
    development, 2/35
    refusal to furnish, 4/73
    re-organization, 4/101
    state militias, 1/14

MINERAL LANDS
    national ownership, 26/83

MINNESOTA
    entered Union, 15/13
    Territory established, 12/16

MINT   See   United States Mint

MISSION TO FRANCE, 2/38
    failure, 2/44

MISSISSIPPI
    Constitution, 18/7, 21, 44
    seceded, 15/17

MISSISSIPPI RIVER
    flood control, 21/63, 73

MISSISSIPPI RIVER COMMISSION,
    21/94

MISSOURI COMPROMISE, 5/18
    constitutionality, 15/11
    extension, 12/22

MIXED CLAIMS COMMISSION
    aliens, 30/115

"MOLLY MAGUIRES", 19/16

MONEY
    Inflation Act, veto, 18/11,
        74
    Public Credit Act, 18/6;
        20/18
    Specie Resumption Act,
        18/13

MONROE DOCTRINE, 5/58
    Adams' part, 6/9
    cardinal to foreign policy,
        26/37
    interpretation, Roosevelt,
        26/9
    President's message to
        Congress, 5/22, 58
    reaffirmed, 11/43; 13/98
    Roosevelt's corollary,
        26/14, 56, 64
    repudiated, 31/11
    Russia's declaration on,
        34/57
    updated, 23/42
    Venezuela, 24/111
    SEE ALSO South American
        Republics

MONTANA
    admitted to Union, 22/16

MORMON CHURCH
    church and state, 15/38
    effect on justice, 20/40
    entered valley of Great
        Salt Lake, 12/10
    polygamy, 20/40

MOROCCO
    declares war, 3/34
    Franco-German mediation,
        26/15

MOSQUITO COAST, 14/57

MOUNTAIN MEADOWS MASSACRE
    Utah, 15/12

MOZAMBIQUE
    independence, 38/42

NICARAGUAN CANAL TREATY
non-ratification, 21/79

NICARAGUAN RECIPROCITY TREATY
approved, 21/140

NILES WEEKLY REGISTER, 9/29

NIPO, CUBA
captured, 25/12

NOBEL PEACE PRIZE
Henry Kissinger, 37/70
Theodore Roosevelt, 26/15
Woodrow Wilson, 28/27

NON-INTERCOURSE ACT, 3/102
repealed, 5/10
revived, 4/50, 52

NORMALCY
no return to, 33/69
after World War 2, 32/200
post-war return to, 29/34,
73

NORRIS-LA GUARDIA BILL See
Labor Laws

NORTH AMERICA
no interference, 11/42

NORTH ATLANTIC TREATY ORGANIZA-
TION
established, 33/32, 33
Europe as part of U. S.
defense, 33/118
French withdrawal, 34/67;
36/46
Germany armed, 34/25
plan to strengthen security,
33/102
troops withdrawn from France,
36/43, 51

NORTH CAROLINA
seceded, 16/15

NORTH DAKOTA
admitted to Union, 22/16

NORTHEASTERN BOUNDARY
dispute, 8/56, 79

NORTH-SOUTH CONTROVERSY, 12/21

NORTHWEST BOUNDARY
settlement, 18/11, 63

NORTHWEST ORDINANCE, 3/54

NORTHWEST TERRITORY
divided, 9/3
slavery, 9/3

NUCLEAR WEAPONS
Army, 34/35
maintenance of deterrent,
37/153
Nuclear Non-Proliferation
Treaty, 37/28, 32
test ban
Russo-U. S. agreement,
35/84
United Nations Nuclear
Non-Proliferation Treaty,
36/62
United States-Russian de-
tente, 36/121

NULLIFICATION, 2/57
Ordinance, 7/54, 59, 71
South Carolina ordinance,
4/27
SEE ALSO Tariffs

O

OCHLOCRACY (GOVERNMENT BY
CROWD), 2/25

OFFICE OF STRATEGIC SERVICES
created, 32/71

OIL AND GAS
Alaska oil pipeline, 37/72;
38/32
dependence on foreign
supplies, 38/175
emergency allocations, 37/74
excise taxes, 38/128
import duties, 38/128
national ownership, 26/97
OPEC raises prices, 38/52
Tidelands Oil Bill, 36/15

OKINAWA
returned to Japan, 37/46

OKLAHOMA
admitted to Union, 26/18

"OLD HICKORY", 7/5

OMNIBUS ACT, 20/16

PROGRESSIVE PARTY
    presidential candidates,
        30/16
    Roosevelt nominated, 26/23;
        27/23

PROHIBITION
    Beer-Wine Revenue Act, 32/23
    Carry Nation's crusade,
        27/14
    Eighteenth Amendment, 28/21,
        23
    repeal opposed, 31/67
    repealed, 32/29
    enforcement problems, 31/13,
        17
    introduced, 29/6
    New York's defiance, 29/14
    pledge to enforce, 30/33,
        40
    ratified, 28/21, 23
    Twenty-first Amendment,
        32/29
    Volstead Act, 28/25
    Wickersham Report, 31/67

PROHIBITION PARTY, 29/5

PUBLIC CREDIT
    first report, 1/33
    Public Credit Act, 18/6
        payment in gold, 20/18

PUBLIC DEPOSITS
    removal to state banks,
        7/74

PUBLIC EFFICIENCY
    Commission on Economy and
        Efficiency, 27/63
    cost of travel, 27/74
    distribution of public
        documents, 27/72
    electricity, 27/73
    indefinite specifications,
        27/73
    mail handling, 27/71

PUBLIC FINANCE
    dollar devalued, 37/50, 53,
        61
    General Appropriations Bill,
        20/21

PUBLIC LANDS
    development of, 26/54

PUBLIC LANDS (Continued)
    sales, 11/70
        withdrawn, 14/45
    unlawful fencing, 26/94

PUBLIC STATUTES See Statutes
    at Large

PUBLIC WELFARE
    children of unemployed
        fathers, 35/99
    Department of Health,
        Education and Welfare
        created, 34/15,92
    Federal Emergency Relief
        Administration created,
        32/25
    Food Stamps fraud, 38/31
        overpayment, 38/102
    Indians, 32/24
    register for jobs and
        training, 37/50
    total reform, 37/116, 129

PUBLIC WORKS
    Civil Works Administration,
        32/29
    Federal Theater, Art, Writers
        projects, 32/39
    Garner-Wagner Bill vetoed,
        32/19
    National Youth Administration,
        32/39,40
    Public Works Administration.
        32/27
    Tennessee Valley Authority,
        32/24
    Works Progress Administration,
        32/31

"PUBLIUS"
    Federalist, 4/6

PUEBLO INCIDENT
    President's statement,
        36/126

PUERTO RICO
    acquired, 25/14
    ceded, 25/13
    Commonwealth status, 33/41
    expedition, 25/12
    Jones Act (Organic Act),
        U.S. citizenship, 28/19
    Spanish relations, 14/26
    U.S. territory, 28/19

R

RECRUITMENT (Continued)
Negroes, 17/10
permanent expansion, 4/101
Selective Service Act,
28/20
Wilson's expansion plan,
28/56
SEE ALSO Military Draft

REFUGEES
Cubans, aided by Immigration
Act, 1965, 36/108
Hungarian refugees admitted,
34/33
Refugee Relief Act, 34/16
SEE ALSO Aliens; Displaced
Persons; Immigration

RELIGIOUS FREEDOM
Virginia Statute, 3/56
SEE ALSO Church and State

REPARATIONS
Germany
default, 30/12
Young Plan, 30/29
one year moratorium, 31/18

REPUBLICAN PARTY
Grand Army of the Republic,
23/20
rift, Taft-Roosevelt, 27/18,
21, 23, 24, 25

REVENUE SHARING
principal purposes, 37/132,
133, 155
state grants, 37/58

REVOLUTIONARY WAR
British surrender, 1/8
SEE ALSO Battles

RHEA LETTER
repudiation, 5/79

RIGHT TO BEAR ARMS, 17/59

RIGHTS OF BRITISH AMERICA,
1774, 3/47

RIOTS
anti-draft, New York, 16/27
anti-war
Chicago, 36/65
Columbia University, 36/60
Kent State, 37/34
New York, 37/35

RIOTS (Continued)
anti-war (continued)
Washington, 37/45
"Bonus Army", Washington,
32/18
Democratic Convention,
Chicago, 36/65
Los Angeles, 34/67
mobs attack Nixon, Caracas,
37/7
mobs, Canal Zone, 36/34
National Guard training,
36/120
Nebraska, cattlemen, 21/62
Panama City, 34/58
"Police Riot", Chicago,
36/68
students' rights, 37/101
SEE ALSO Race and Race
Relations

RIVERS AND HARBORS ACT
vetoed, 21/64, 101

ROUGH RIDERS
Theodore Roosevelt's ser-
vice, 26/7

"RUM, ROMANISM AND REBELLION",
21/77

RUSH-BAGOT AGREEMENT
Great Lakes, disarmament,
5/14

RUSSIA
Alaska Treaty, 17/24
claims, Pacific Coast, 5/21
Commercial Treaty, 15/5
Iran occupied by, 33/19
Lend-lease Agreement, 32/80
Nixon's address to Russians,
37/163
Nuclear Test Ban Agreement,
35/84
recognized, 32/29
revolution begun, 28/19
support for Arabs in Middle
East, 36/52
world domination, 33/117,
126
SEE ALSO Cold War; Hot Line;
Iran; Monroe Doctrine

S

SAC INDIANS   See   Indian Tribes
(American)

SAFETY
Coal Mine Health and Safety
Act, 37/29
Occupational Health and
Safety Act, 37/43
SEE ALSO Health

ST. LAWRENCE RIVER
navigation, 14/41, 18/47

"SALARY GRAB ACT", 20/21

SAMOA   See   American Samoa

SAN FRANCISCO EARTHQUAKE, 26/16

SAN JUAN HILL, 26/7

SANTIAGO, CUBA
naval blockade, 25/11
surrender, 23/27; 25/12

SANTO DOMINGO   See   Dominican
Republic

SAVANNAH
first Atlantic crossing,
5/18

SCANDALS
Adams (Sherman), resignation,
34/42
air mail contracts, 32/31
armor plate fraud, 24/24
Baker (Bobby), Secretary of
Senate, 36/32, 35
bribery, 29/16
Credit Mobilier, 18/11;
20/18, 20, 21
Douglas (Justice William O.),
charged unethical conduct,
37/34, 42
electric power, conflict of
interest, 34/21
Elk Hills, oil lease, 30/19
Fortas (Abe), resignation
from Supreme Court, 37/20
Fulbright Report, 33/39
Harding administration,
29/15

SCANDALS (Continued)
Harding administration,
Hoover's comment, 29/16
My Lai massacre, information
suppressed, 37/33
Nixon-Douglas (Helen G.)
election, 37/4
Nixon's secret election
fund, 37/5
oil, Senate hearings, 29/16
oil, Sinclair jailed, 30/24
"Teapot Dome", 27/29; 29/11;
30/26
Texas senatorial election,
36/10
Veterans Bureau, investigat-
ion, 29/13,14,60; 30/11,
15
West Point, 38/78, 88
SEE ALSO Corruption; Watergate

SCOTTSBORO CASE
retrial, Alabama rape case,
31/26

SEARCH AND SEIZURE, 30/70

SECESSION
Lincoln's First Inaugural,
16/106
right of denied, 15/70
states
Alabama, 15/17
Arkansas, 16/15
Florida, 15/17
Georgia, 15/17
Louisiana, 15/17
Mississippi, 15/17
South Carolina, 10/74
Tennessee, 16/15; 17/5
Texas, 15/17
Virginia, 10/75

SECOND BANK OF THE UNITED STATES
recharter vetoed, 7/45, 74,
80

SECRETARY OF WAR
insubordination, 17/25

SECURITIES AND EXCHANGE
COMMISSION, 32/34
Chairmen, 32/36, 42
SEE ALSO Finance

SEDITION ACT See Alien and
Sedition Acts

SELECTIVE SERVICE ACT See
Military Draft

SEMINOLE INDIANS See Indian
Tribes (American)

SENECA INDIANS See Indian
Tribes (American)

SHAWNEE INDIANS See Indian
Tribes (American)

SHERMAN ANTI-TRUST ACT, 23/20
ambiguity, 23/58
SEE ALSO Trusts and Monopolies

SHERMAN SILVER PURCHASE ACT,
23/60
repealed, 24/23

SHIPS AND SHIPPING
foreign interference, 3/84,
91
ships, seizure by France,
2/31

SHOSHONEE INDIANS See Indian
Tribes (American)

SILVER
Bimetallism agreements,
25/9,20
Bland-Allison Act limiting
purchases, 19/19, 46
Bullion Coinage Bill,
24/101
free silver coinage, 19/37
Sherman Silver Purchase
Act, 23/20, 60
repealed, 24/23

SIOUX INDIANS See Indian
Tribes (American)

SLAVE TRADE
abolished in District of
Columbia, 1850, 13/59
Convention rejected by
Senate, 6/10
denunciation, 4/52
importation banned, 3/42
suppression, 8/107; 16/20
United States participation,
12/31

SLAVE TRADE (Continued)
Wanderer, 15/51
Webster Ashburton Treaty,
10/105
SEE ALSO Slavery

SLAVERY
agitation condemned, 15/11
emancipation, Columbus
Speech, 16/76
Final Public Address,
Lincoln, 16/130
gradual, 16/20
ended, District of Columbia,
16/20
insurrection, South
Carolina, 5/20
Jefferson's views, 3/109
Lincoln's early views,
16/49
Missouri Compromise, 5/18
No interference, nine
states' resolve, 12/22
return to Africa, 5/38
states' rights, 14/3, 17
Thirteenth Amendment, 16/39
Underground Railroad, 19/3
Union, paramount object,
16/23
SEE ALSO Abolition; Dred
Scott Decision; Emancipation
Proclamation; Free Soil
Party; Fugitive Slave Act;
L'Amistad Case; Slave Trade

SLIDELL MISSION
Boundaries, U.S.-Mexico,
15/8

SOCIAL SECURITY
benefits
coverage, 33/98
extended, 35/10; 37/72
taxes, 37/58
tied to cost of living,
37/55
Franklin Delano Roosevelt,
1935, 32/38
Medicare, 36/103
millions not covered, 34/89
pensions, unemployment
insurance, 32/40
provision of hospital care,
36/91
Social Security Act, 32/40

"TEAPOT DOME" See Scandals

TEHERAN CONFERENCE, 32/88

TELEGRAPH
    invention, 16/36

TELEPHONE EXCHANGE
    first, New Haven, 19/19

TELEVISION
    attack on news coverage,
        37/27
    Federal Communications Com-
        mission supervision,
        34/56
    first Presidential appear-
        ance, 32/56
    first telecast, 31/10
    Kennedy-Nixon debates,
        34/59; 37/9
    Nixon's "Checkers" speech,
        37/5
    Watergate, Senate Committee
        hearings, 37/65

TENNESSEE
    Constitutional Convention,
        17/13
    Johnson's military rule,
        17/6, 7, 8, 9
    re-admitted, 17/21
    secession, 16/15, 17/5

TENNESSEE VALLEY AUTHORITY
    Act signed, 32/25
    request for, 32/24

TENURE OF OFFICE ACT, 22/39

TERRITORIAL ACQUISITION,
    14/9, 28, 68
    adjacent territories, 17/60
    Mariana Islands, 38/41
    Midway Island, 17/25
    two hundred mile sea border,
        38/73

TERRITORIES
    early statehood advocated,
        23/42

TERRORISM
    Athens airport, 36/69
    federal armed guards, 37/39
    La Guardia airport, eleven
        killed, 38/62

TERRORISM (Continued)
    plane hijacked to Uganda,
        38/83
    Israel frees hostages,
        38/84

TEXAS
    annexation, 10/70, 71, 113,
        117, 123, 126; 11/32, 35;
        15/7
    boundary dispute, 11/10;
        21/72
    treaty, 8/15
    Constitution, 11/35; 18/7,
        21, 44
    independence recognized,
        7/18, 110
    reunion, 11/31
    seceded, 15/17
    Seed Bill vetoed, 22/61

THAILAND
    troops in, 35/12

THANKSGIVING PROCLAMATION
    first, 1/32

TIPPECANOE
    report on battle, 9/15

TRADE UNIONS
    Boston police, 30/5
    Congress of Industrial Or-
        ganizations (CIO) formed,
        32/42
    right to join, 32/40
    United Mine Workers, 30/68
    SEE ALSO Labor Disputes;
        Labor Laws; Labor Violence

TRADING WITH THE ENEMY ACT,
    28/21

TRANSPORTATION
    common carriers, supervision
        of, 26/83
    coordination required,
        29/102
    Department of Transportation
        created, 36/47, 115
    federal aid, mass transit,
        37/40
    federal coordinator appoin-
        ted, 32/26
    high-speed rail tests,
        36/90
    highway transit fund, use
        for mass transit, 37/68

VIETNAM
   defense aid pledged,   35/11
   Democratic Republic
      created,   33/15
   financial aid,   34/24
   Fulbright Senate hearings,
      36/45, 56, 57
   Geneva Declaration, divi-
      sion at 17th parallel,
      36/17
   United States pledges fur-
      ther aid,   35/38

VIETNAM WAR
   anti-war demonstrations
      Chicago,   36/65
      Kent State,   37/34
      New York,   36/60
      Washington,   37/27, 45
   bombing halt ordered,
      36/134
   clemency program ends,
      38/34
   colleges closed,   37/35
   domino theory, belief in,
      35/93
   end of war, 1973.   37/188
      191; 38/36
   French surrender, Dienbien-
      phu,   34/19
   growing American involve-
      ment, 1963,   35/91
   hawks and doves, long
      national debate,   36/45
   last United States troops
      leave,   37/56
   My Lai massacre,   37/33
   opportunities to negotiate
      neglected,   36/95
   Tonkin Gulf incident,
      36/37, 86
   United Nations admission
      prevented, by United
      States,   38/52
   United States Military Com-
      mand established,   35/11
   United States troops with-
      drawal,   37/29, 40, 45,
      51, 56

VIOLENCE IN AMERICA
   Commission on Violence ap-
      pointed,   36/130
   SEE ALSO Assassination; Riots

VIRGIN ISLANDS
   purchased,   28/18
   Treaty with Denmark,   17/25,
      60

VIRGINIA
   Constitution,   18/21
   Convention,   3/7
   notes on,   3/53
   religious freedom in,   3/56
   seceded,   10/75; 16/15
   University opened,   3/45

VIRGINIA COLONIZATION SOCIETY,
   10/65

VIRGINIA RESOLUTIONS   See
   Kentucky and Virginia Resolutions

VIRGINIUS AFFAIR
   capture by Spain,   18/78
   SEE ALSO Spain

VOLSTEAD ACT   See   Prohibition

VOTING RIGHTS See   Suffrage

W

WAGES AND HOURS
   eight-hour day,   26/8, 80;
      28/17
   forty-hour week,   32/44
   half holidays,   26/81
   minimum wage,   32/48
      Act,   36/48
      declared,   33/34
      increased,   37/75
      law expanded,   35/9
   railroad labor,   26/72
   wage and price controls,
      37/65, 140
   wage freeze,   37/48
      post-freeze control,
      37/142, 147
   wage restraint, construc-
      tion industries,   37/44

WAKE ISLAND
   claimed,   25/15

WALKER TARIFF
   duties reduced,   11/15

WANDERER
   importation of slaves,   15/51

WAR CRIMES
   German concentration camps,
      34/7
   Nuremberg trials,   33/16

WAR DEBTS
  liquidation, 30/33, 59, 76
  one-year moratorium, 31/18
  terms, Great Britain, 29/14

WAR POWERS
  Constitution, 15/54

WAR SHIPPING ADMINISTRATION
  created, 32/78

WARREN COMMISSION, 36/33, 38,
  74; 38/4

WARS
  Angola, 38/57
  Black Hawk War, 12/5
  Civil War (U.S.) See Civil
    War
  Dey of Algiers, declara-
    tion, 4/25
  France, 2/44
    special message to Con-
      gress, 2/31
    avoided, 2/67, 76
  German record, 32/177
  Great Britain, 1812, 3/43
    Battle of the Thames, 9/7
    Fort Meigs, 9/7
    Naval battle, Lake Erie,
      9/7
  Israeli-Arab, 33/28
    1967, 36/52
  Italian record, 32/177
  Italy-Ethiopia, 32/42
  Japanese record, 32/177
  Lebanon, 38/64
  Nigerian Civil War, 36/64
  North Korea invasion, 33/35
  Spanish American See Spain,
    war with
  Spanish Civil War, 32/47
  Vietnam
    Cambodia invaded, 38/7
    ends, 38/36, 37
    President's review, 38/133
  War of Independence See
  Revolutionary War
  SEE ALSO Battles; War Crimes

WASHINGTON, D. C.
  burned by British, 4/23;
    5/12
  master plan, 1/12

WASHINGTON (STATE)
  admitted to Union, 22/16

WASHINGTON (TERRITORY)
  boundary dispute, 14/26,
    42, 60

WATERGATE
  break-in, Mitchell's
    denial, 37/67
  burglars indicted, 37/57,
    60, 63
  burglars seized, 37/54
  burglary, Democratic
    headquarters, 38/8
  conspirators convicted,
    38/26
  cover-up conspiracy,
    37/55, 57, 64, 78, 79
  Cox (Archibald), special
    prosecutor, 37/66;
    38/9
  Dean (John W.) sentenced,
    37/78
    testimony, 37/66
  Ervin Senate Committee
    hearings, 37/61
  Federal Bureau of Investi-
    gation, sensitive papers
    destroyed, 37/64
  impeachment See Impeach-
    ment, Nixon
  Nixon, Richard M.
    declares innocence,
      37/62, 66
    radio defense, 37/197
    resignation, 37/78;
      38/12
    television denial, 37/68
  Presidential aides indicted,
    37/74
  relation to National Secur-
    ity, 37/203
  release tapes, Judge Sirica,
    37/69, 70
  resignation of Ehrlichman,
    Haldeman, Dean, 38/9
  Saturday Night massacre,
    37/70; 38/10
  sentencings, 37/63, 71,
    76, 77
  Supreme Court ruling to
    turn over tapes, 37/77
  tapes, edited transcripts,
    37/75
    erasures, 37/71, 73
    President's knowledge,
      37/62

X
Y
Z

XYZ AFFAIR, 2/11, 12, 44, 46
   papers released to Congress,
      3/23

YALTA
   Russian violation, 33/12
   Yalta Conference, 32/95,96
   SEE ALSO World War 2

YELLOWSTONE NATIONAL PARK
   opened, 21/70

YORKTOWN
   surrender centennial, 21/59

YOUNG PLAN, 30/29

DOCUMENTS
The Presidents and Their Administrations

DOCUMENTS

EXECUTIVE OFFICERS, 1789-1977

First Administration of GEORGE WASHINGTON

APRIL 30, 1789, TO MARCH 3, 1793

PRESIDENT OF THE UNITED STATES—GEORGE WASHINGTON, of Virginia.

VICE PRESIDENT OF THE UNITED STATES—JOHN ADAMS, of Massachusetts.

SECRETARY OF STATE—JOHN JAY, of New York, was Secretary for Foreign Affairs under the Confederation, and continued to act, at the request of Washington, until Jefferson took office. THOMAS JEFFERSON, of Virginia, September 26, 1789; entered upon duties March 22, 1790.

SECRETARY OF THE TREASURY—ALEXANDER HAMILTON, of New York, September 11, 1789.

SECRETARY OF WAR—HENRY KNOX, of Massachusetts, September 12, 1789.

ATTORNEY GENERAL—EDMUND RANDOLPH, of Virginia, September 26, 1789; entered upon duties February 2, 1790.

POSTMASTER GENERAL—SAMUEL OSGOOD, of Massachusetts, September 26, 1789. TIMOTHY PICKERING, of Pennsylvania, August 12, 1791; entered upon duties August 19, 1791.

Second Administration of GEORGE WASHINGTON

MARCH 4, 1793, TO MARCH 3, 1797

PRESIDENT OF THE UNITED STATES—GEORGE WASHINGTON, of Virginia.

VICE PRESIDENT OF THE UNITED STATES—JOHN ADAMS, of Massachusetts.

SECRETARY OF STATE—THOMAS JEFFERSON, of Virginia, continued from preceding administration. EDMUND RANDOLPH, of Virginia, January 2, 1794. TIMOTHY PICKERING, of Pennsylvania (Secretary of War), ad interim, August 20, 1795. TIMOTHY PICKERING, of Pennsylvania, December 10, 1795.

SECRETARY OF THE TREASURY—ALEXANDER HAMILTON, of New York, continued from preceding administration. OLIVER WOLCOTT, Jr., of Connecticut, February 2, 1795.

SECRETARY OF WAR—HENRY KNOX, of Massachusetts, continued from preceding administration. TIMOTHY PICKERING, of Pennsylvania, January 2, 1795. TIMOTHY PICKERING, of Pennsylvania (Secretary of State), ad interim, December 10, 1795, to February 5, 1796. JAMES MCHENRY, of Maryland, January 27, 1796; entered upon duties February 6, 1796.

ATTORNEY GENERAL—EDMUND RANDOLPH, of Virginia, continued from preceding administration. WILLIAM BRADFORD, of Pennsylvania, January 27, 1794; entered upon duties January 29, 1794. CHARLES LEE, of Virginia, December 10, 1795.

POSTMASTER GENERAL—TIMOTHY PICKERING, of Pennsylvania, continued from preceding administration. TIMOTHY PICKERING, of Pennsylvania, recommissioned June 1, 1794. JOSEPH HABERSHAM, of Georgia, February 25, 1795.

Administration of JOHN ADAMS

MARCH 4, 1797, TO MARCH 3, 1801

PRESIDENT OF THE UNITED STATES—JOHN ADAMS, of Massachusetts.

VICE PRESIDENT OF THE UNITED STATES—THOMAS JEFFERSON, of Virginia.

SECRETARY OF STATE—TIMOTHY PICKERING, of Pennsylvania, continued from preceding administration; resignation requested May 10, 1800, but declining to resign, he was dismissed May 12, 1800. CHARLES LEE, of Virginia (Attorney General), ad interim, May 13, 1800. JOHN MARSHALL, of Virginia, May 13, 1800; entered upon duties June 6, 1800. John Marshall, of Virginia (Chief Justice of the United States), ad interim, February 4, 1801, to March 3, 1801.

SECRETARY OF THE TREASURY—OLIVER WOLCOTT, Jr., of Connecticut, continued from preceding administration. SAMUEL DEXTER, of Massachusetts, January 1, 1801.

SECRETARY OF WAR—JAMES McHENRY, of Maryland, continued from preceding administration. BENJAMIN STODDERT, of Maryland (Secretary of the Navy), ad interim, June 1, 1800, to June 12, 1800. SAMUEL DEXTER, of Massachusetts, May 13, 1800; entered upon duties June 12, 1800. SAMUEL DEXTER, of Massachusetts (Secretary of the Treasury), ad interim, January 1, 1801.

ATTORNEY GENERAL—CHARLES LEE, of Virginia, continued from preceding administration.

POSTMASTER GENERAL—JOSEPH HABERSHAM, of Georgia, continued from preceding administration.

SECRETARY OF THE NAVY—BENJAMIN STODDERT, of Maryland, May 21, 1798; entered upon duties June 18, 1798.

First Administration of THOMAS JEFFERSON

MARCH 4, 1801, TO MARCH 3, 1805

PRESIDENT OF THE UNITED STATES—THOMAS JEFFERSON, of Virginia.

VICE PRESIDENT OF THE UNITED STATES—AARON BURR, of New York.

SECRETARY OF STATE—JOHN MARSHALL, of Virginia (Chief Justice of the United States), for one day (March 4, 1801), and for a special purpose. LEVI LINCOLN, of Massachusetts (Attorney General), ad interim, March 5, 1801. JAMES MADISON, of Virginia, March 5, 1801; entered upon duties May 2, 1801.

SECRETARY OF THE TREASURY—SAMUEL DEXTER, of Massachusetts, continued from preceding administration to May 6, 1801, ALBERT GALLATIN, of Pennsylvania, May 14, 1801.

SECRETARY OF WAR—HENRY DEARBORN, of Massachusetts, March 5, 1801.

ATTORNEY GENERAL—LEVI LINCOLN, of Massachusetts, March 5, 1801, to December 31, 1804.

POSTMASTER GENERAL—JOSEPH HABERSHAM, of Georgia, continued from preceding administration. GIDEON GRANGER, of Connecticut, November 28, 1801.

SECRETARY OF THE NAVY—BENJAMIN STODDERT, of Maryland, continued from preceding administration. HENRY DEARBORN, of Massachusetts (Secretary of War), ad interim, April 1, 1801. ROBERT SMITH, of Maryland, July 15, 1801; entered upon duties July 27, 1801.

Second Administration of THOMAS JEFFERSON

MARCH 4, 1805, TO MARCH 3, 1809

PRESIDENT OF THE UNITED STATES—THOMAS JEFFERSON, of Virginia.

VICE PRESIDENT OF THE UNITED STATES—GEORGE CLINTON, of New York.

SECRETARY OF STATE—JAMES MADISON, of Virginia, continued from preceding administration.

SECRETARY OF THE TREASURY—ALBERT GALLATIN, of Pennsylvania, continued from preceding administration.

SECRETARY OF WAR—HENRY DEARBORN, of Massachusetts, continued from preceding administration. JOHN SMITH (chief clerk), ad interim, February 17, 1809.

ATTORNEY GENERAL—JOHN BRECKENRIDGE, of Kentucky, August 7, 1805 (died December 14, 1806). CÆSAR A. RODNEY, of Delaware, January 20, 1807.

POSTMASTER GENERAL—GIDEON GRANGER, of Connecticut, continued from preceding administration.

SECRETARY OF THE NAVY—ROBERT SMITH, of Maryland, continued from preceding administration.

First Administration of JAMES MADISON

MARCH 4, 1809, TO MARCH 3, 1813

PRESIDENT OF THE UNITED STATES—James Madison, of Virginia.

VICE PRESIDENT OF THE UNITED STATES—George Clinton, of New York. (Died April 20, 1812.)

PRESIDENT PRO TEMPORE OF THE SENATE—William H. Crawford, of Georgia.

SECRETARY OF STATE—Robert Smith, of Maryland, March 6, 1809. James Monroe, of Virginia, April 2, 1811; entered upon duties April 6, 1811.

SECRETARY OF THE TREASURY—Albert Gallatin, of Pennsylvania, continued from preceding administration.

SECRETARY OF WAR—John Smith (chief clerk), ad interim, continued from preceding administration. William Eustis, of Massachusetts, March 7, 1809; entered upon duties April 8, 1809; served to December 31, 1812. James Monroe, of Virginia (Secretary of State), ad interim, January 1, 1813. John Armstrong, of New York, January 13, 1813; entered upon duties February 5, 1813.

ATTORNEY GENERAL—Cæsar A. Rodney, of Delaware, continued from preceding administration; resigned December 5, 1811. William Pinkney, of Maryland, December 11, 1811; entered upon duties January 6, 1812.

POSTMASTER GENERAL—Gideon Granger, of Connecticut, continued from preceding administration.

SECRETARY OF THE NAVY—Robert Smith, of Maryland, continued from preceding administration. Charles W. Goldsborough (chief clerk), ad interim, March 8, 1809. Paul Hamilton, of South Carolina, March 7, 1809; entered upon duties May 15, 1809; served to December 31, 1812. Charles W. Goldsborough (chief clerk), ad interim, January 7, 1813, to January 18, 1813. William Jones, of Pennsylvania, January 12, 1813; entered upon duties January 19, 1813.

Second Administration of JAMES MADISON

MARCH 4, 1813, TO MARCH 3, 1817

PRESIDENT OF THE UNITED STATES—James Madison, of Virginia.

VICE PRESIDENT OF THE UNITED STATES—Elbridge Gerry, of Massachusetts. (Died November 23, 1814.)

PRESIDENT PRO TEMPORE OF THE SENATE—John Gaillard, of South Carolina.

SECRETARY OF STATE—James Monroe, of Virginia, continued from preceding administration. James Monroe, of Virginia (Secretary of War), ad interim, October 1, 1814. James Monroe, of Virginia, February 28, 1815.

SECRETARY OF THE TREASURY—Albert Gallatin, of Pennsylvania, continued from preceding administration. William Jones, of Pennsylvania (Secretary of the Navy), performed the duties of the Secretary of the Treasury during the absence of Mr. Gallatin in Europe (April 21, 1813, to February 9, 1814). George W. Campbell, of Tennessee, February 9, 1814. Alexander J. Dallas, of Pennsylvania, October 6, 1814; entered upon duties October 14, 1814. William H. Crawford, of Georgia, October 22, 1816.

SECRETARY OF WAR—John Armstrong, of New York, continued from preceding administration. James Monroe, of Virginia (Secretary of State), ad interim, August 30, 1814. James Monroe, of Virginia, September 27, 1814; entered upon duties October 1, 1814. James Monroe, of Virginia (Secretary of State), ad interim, March 1, 1815. Alexander J. Dallas, of Pennsylvania (Secretary of the Treasury), ad interim, March 14, 1815, to August 8, 1815. William H. Crawford, of Georgia, August 1, 1815; entered upon duties August 8, 1815. George Graham (chief clerk), ad interim, October 22, 1816, to close of administration.

ATTORNEY GENERAL—William Pinkney, of Maryland, continued from preceding administration. Richard Rush, of Pennsylvania, February 10, 1814; entered upon duties the day following.

POSTMASTER GENERAL—Gideon Granger, of Connecticut, continued from preceding administration. Return J. Meigs, Jr., of Ohio, March 17, 1814; entered upon duties April 11, 1814.

SECRETARY OF THE NAVY—William Jones, of Pennsylvania, continued from preceding administration. Benjamin Homans (chief clerk), ad interim, December 2, 1814. Benjamin W. Crowninshield, of Massachusetts, December 19, 1814; entered upon duties January 16, 1815.

First Administration of JAMES MONROE

MARCH 4, 1817, TO MARCH 3, 1821

PRESIDENT OF THE UNITED STATES—James Monroe, of Virginia.

VICE PRESIDENT OF THE UNITED STATES—Daniel D. Tompkins, of New York.

SECRETARY OF STATE—John Graham (chief clerk), ad interim, March 4, 1817. Richard Rush, of Pennsylvania (Attorney General), ad interim, March 10, 1817. John Quincy Adams, of Massachusetts, March 5, 1817; entered upon duties September 22, 1817.

SECRETARY OF THE TREASURY—William H. Crawford, of Georgia, continued from preceding administration. William H. Crawford, of Georgia, recommissioned March 5, 1817.

SECRETARY OF WAR—George Graham (chief clerk), ad interim, March 4, 1817. John C. Calhoun, of South Carolina, October 8, 1817; entered upon duties December 10, 1817.

ATTORNEY GENERAL—Richard Rush, of Pennsylvania, continued from preceding administration to October 30, 1817. William Wirt, of Virginia, November 13, 1817; entered upon duties November 15, 1817.

POSTMASTER GENERAL—Return J. Meigs, Jr., of Ohio, continued from preceding administration.

SECRETARY OF THE NAVY—Benjamin W. Crowninshield, of Massachusetts, continued from preceding administration. John C. Calhoun, of South Carolina (Secretary of War), ad interim, October 1, 1818. Smith Thompson, of New York, November 9, 1818; entered upon duties January 1, 1819.

Second Administration of JAMES MONROE

MARCH 4, 1821, TO MARCH 3, 1825

PRESIDENT OF THE UNITED STATES—James Monroe, of Virginia.

VICE PRESIDENT OF THE UNITED STATES—Daniel D. Tompkins, of New York.

SECRETARY OF STATE—John Quincy Adams, of Massachusetts, continued from preceding administration.

SECRETARY OF THE TREASURY—William H. Crawford, of Georgia, continued from preceding administration.

SECRETARY OF WAR—John C. Calhoun, of South Carolina, continued from preceding administration.

ATTORNEY GENERAL—William Wirt, of Virginia, continued from preceding administration.

POSTMASTER GENERAL—Return J. Meigs, Jr., of Ohio, continued from preceding administration. John McLean, of Ohio, commissioned June 26, 1823, to take effect July 1, 1823.

SECRETARY OF THE NAVY—Smith Thompson, of New York, continued from preceding administration. John Rodgers (commodore, United States Navy, and President of the Board of Navy Commissioners), ad interim, September 1, 1823. Samuel L. Southard, of New Jersey, September 16, 1823.

Administration of JOHN QUINCY ADAMS

MARCH 4, 1825, TO MARCH 3, 1829

PRESIDENT OF THE UNITED STATES—John Quincy Adams, of Massachusetts.

VICE PRESIDENT OF THE UNITED STATES—John. C. Calhoun, of South Carolina.

SECRETARY OF STATE—Daniel Brent (chief clerk), ad interim, March 4, 1825. Henry Clay, of Kentucky, March 7, 1825.

SECRETARY OF THE TREASURY—Samuel L. Southard, of New Jersey (Secretary of the Navy), ad interim, March 7, 1825. Richard Rush, of Pennsylvania, March 7, 1825; entered upon duties August 1, 1825.

SECRETARY OF WAR—James Barbour, of Virginia, March 7, 1825. Samuel L. Southard, of New Jersey (Secretary of the Navy), ad interim, May 26, 1828. Peter B. Porter, of New York, May 26, 1828; entered upon duties June 21, 1828.

ATTORNEY GENERAL—William Wirt, of Virginia, continued from preceding administration.

POSTMASTER GENERAL—John McLean, of Ohio, continued from preceding administration.

SECRETARY OF THE NAVY—Samuel L. Southard, of New Jersey, continued from preceding administration.

First Administration of ANDREW JACKSON

MARCH 4, 1829, TO MARCH 3, 1833

PRESIDENT OF THE UNITED STATES—ANDREW JACKSON, of Tennessee.

VICE PRESIDENT OF THE UNITED STATES—JOHN C. CALHOUN, of South Carolina. (Resigned December 28, 1832.)

PRESIDENT PRO TEMPORE OF THE SENATE—HUGH LAWSON WHITE, of Tennessee.

SECRETARY OF STATE—JAMES A. HAMILTON, of New York, ad interim, March 4, 1829. MARTIN VAN BUREN, of New York, March 6, 1829; entered upon duties March 28, 1829. EDWARD LIVINGSTON, of Louisiana, May 24, 1831.

SECRETARY OF THE TREASURY—SAMUEL D. INGHAM, of Pennsylvania, March 6, 1829. ASBURY DICKINS (chief clerk), ad interim, June 21, 1831. LOUIS MCLANE, of Delaware, August 8, 1831.

SECRETARY OF WAR—JOHN H. EATON, of Tennessee, March 9, 1829. PHILIP G. RANDOLPH (chief clerk), ad interim, June 20, 1831. ROGER B. TANEY, of Maryland (Attorney General), ad interim, July 21, 1831. LEWIS CASS, of Ohio, August 1, 1831; entered upon duties August 8, 1831.

ATTORNEY GENERAL—JOHN M. BERRIEN, of Georgia, March 9, 1829, to June 22, 1831. ROGER B. TANEY, of Maryland, July 20, 1831.

POSTMASTER GENERAL—JOHN MCLEAN, of Ohio, continued from preceding administration. WILLIAM T. BARRY, of Kentucky, March 9, 1829; entered upon duties April 6, 1829.

SECRETARY OF THE NAVY—CHARLES HAY (chief clerk), ad interim, March 4, 1829. JOHN BRANCH, of North Carolina, March 9, 1829. JOHN BOYLE (chief clerk), ad interim, May 12, 1831. LEVI WOODBURY, of New Hampshire, May 23, 1831.

Second Administration of ANDREW JACKSON

MARCH 4, 1833, TO MARCH 3, 1837

PRESIDENT OF THE UNITED STATES—ANDREW JACKSON, of Tennessee.

VICE PRESIDENT OF THE UNITED STATES—MARTIN VAN BUREN, of New York.

SECRETARY OF STATE—EDWARD LIVINGSTON, of Louisiana, continued from preceding administration. LOUIS MCLANE, of Delaware, May 29, 1833. JOHN FORSYTH, of Georgia, June 27, 1834; entered upon duties July 1, 1834.

SECRETARY OF THE TREASURY—LOUIS MCLANE, of Delaware, continued from preceding administration. WILLIAM J. DUANE, of Pennsylvania, May 29, 1833; entered upon duties June 1, 1833. ROGER B. TANEY, of Maryland, September 23, 1833. MCCLINTOCK YOUNG (chief clerk), ad interim, June 25, 1834. LEVI WOODBURY, of New Hampshire, June 27, 1834; entered upon duties July 1, 1834.

SECRETARY OF WAR—LEWIS CASS, of Ohio, continued from preceding administration. CAREY A. HARRIS, of Tennessee (Commissioner of Indian Affairs), ad interim, October 5, 1836. BENJAMIN F. BUTLER, of New York (Attorney General), ad interim, October 26, 1836. BENJAMIN F. BUTLER, of New York, commissioned March 3, 1837, ad interim, "during the pleasure of the President, until a successor, duly appointed, shall accept such office and enter upon the duties thereof."

ATTORNEY GENERAL—ROGER B. TANEY, of Maryland, continued from preceding administration to September 23, 1833. BENJAMIN F. BUTLER, of New York, November 15, 1833; entered upon duties November 18, 1833.

POSTMASTER GENERAL—WILLIAM T. BARRY, of Kentucky, continued from preceding administration. AMOS KENDALL, of Kentucky, May 1, 1835.

SECRETARY OF THE NAVY—LEVI WOODBURY, of New Hampshire, continued from preceding administration. MAHLON DICKERSON, of New Jersey, June 30, 1834.

Administration of MARTIN VAN BUREN

MARCH 4, 1837, TO MARCH 3, 1841

PRESIDENT OF THE UNITED STATES—MARTIN VAN BUREN, of New York.

VICE PRESIDENT OF THE UNITED STATES—RICHARD M. JOHNSON, of Kentucky.

SECRETARY OF STATE—JOHN FORSYTH, of Georgia, continued from preceding administration.

SECRETARY OF THE TREASURY—LEVI WOODBURY, of New Hampshire, continued from preceding administration.

SECRETARY OF WAR—BENJAMIN F. BUTLER, of New York, ad interim, continued from preceding administration. JOEL R. POINSETT, of South Carolina, March 7, 1837; entered upon duties March 14, 1837.

ATTORNEY GENERAL—BENJAMIN F. BUTLER, of New York, continued from preceding administration. FELIX GRUNDY, of Tennessee, July 5, 1838, to take effect September 1, 1838. HENRY D. GILPIN, of Pennsylvania, January 11, 1840.

POSTMASTER GENERAL—AMOS KENDALL, of Kentucky, continued from preceding administration. JOHN M. NILES, of Connecticut, May 19, 1840, to take effect May 25, 1840; entered upon duties May 26, 1840.

SECRETARY OF THE NAVY—MAHLON DICKERSON, of New Jersey, continued from preceding administration. JAMES K. PAULDING, of New York, June 25, 1838, to take effect "after the 30th instant"; entered upon duties July 1, 1838.

Administration of WILLIAM HENRY HARRISON

MARCH 4, 1841, TO APRIL 4, 1841

PRESIDENT OF THE UNITED STATES—WILLIAM HENRY HARRISON, of Ohio. (Died April 4, 1841.)

VICE PRESIDENT OF THE UNITED STATES—JOHN TYLER, of Virginia.

SECRETARY OF STATE—J. L. MARTIN (chief clerk), ad interim, March 4, 1841. DANIEL WEBSTER, of Massachusetts, March 5, 1841.

SECRETARY OF THE TREASURY—MCCLINTOCK YOUNG (chief clerk), ad interim, March 4, 1841. THOMAS EWING, of Ohio, March 5, 1841.

SECRETARY OF WAR—JOHN BELL, of Tennessee, March 5, 1841.

ATTORNEY GENERAL—JOHN J. CRITTENDEN, of Kentucky, March 5, 1841.

POSTMASTER GENERAL—SELAH R. HOBBIE, of New York (First Assistant Postmaster General), ad interim, March 4, 1841. FRANCIS GRANGER, of New York, March 6, 1841; entered upon duties March 8, 1841.

SECRETARY OF THE NAVY—JOHN D. SIMMS (chief clerk), ad interim, March 4, 1841. GEORGE E. BADGER, of North Carolina, March 5, 1841.

Administration of JOHN TYLER

APRIL 6, 1841, TO MARCH 3, 1845

PRESIDENT OF THE UNITED STATES—JOHN TYLER, of Virginia.

PRESIDENT PRO TEMPORE OF THE SENATE—SAMUEL L. SOUTHARD, of New Jersey; WILLIE P. MANGUM, of North Carolina.

SECRETARY OF STATE—DANIEL WEBSTER, of Massachusetts, continued from preceding administration. HUGH S. LEGARÉ, of South Carolina (Attorney General), ad interim, May 9, 1843. WILLIAM S. DERRICK (chief clerk), ad interim, June 21, 1843. ABEL P. UPSHUR, of Virginia (Secretary of the Navy), ad interim, June 24, 1843. ABEL P. UPSHUR, of Virginia, July 24, 1843 (killed by the explosion of a gun on the U. S. S. *Princeton* February 28, 1844). JOHN NELSON, of Maryland (Attorney General), ad interim, February 29, 1844. JOHN C. CALHOUN, of South Carolina, March 6, 1844; entered upon duties April 1, 1844.

SECRETARY OF THE TREASURY—THOMAS EWING, of Ohio, continued from preceding administration. MCCLINTOCK YOUNG (chief clerk), ad interim, September 13, 1841. WALTER FORWARD, of Pennsylvania, September 13, 1841. MCCLINTOCK YOUNG (chief clerk), ad interim, March 1, 1843. JOHN C. SPENCER, of New York, March 3, 1843; entered upon duties March 8, 1843. MCCLINTOCK YOUNG (chief clerk), ad interim, May 2, 1844. GEORGE M. BIBB, of Kentucky, June 15, 1844; entered upon duties July 4, 1844.

SECRETARY OF WAR—JOHN BELL, of Tennessee, continued from preceding administration. ALBERT M. LEA, of Maryland (chief clerk), ad interim, September 12, 1841. JOHN C. SPENCER, of New York, October 12, 1841. JAMES M. PORTER, of Pennsylvania, March 8, 1843. WILLIAM WILKINS, of Pennsylvania, February 15, 1844; entered upon duties February 20, 1844.

ATTORNEY GENERAL—JOHN J. CRITTENDEN, of Kentucky, continued from preceding administration. HUGH S. LEGARÉ, of South Carolina, September 13, 1841; entered upon duties September 20, 1841 (died June 20, 1843). JOHN NELSON, of Maryland, July 1, 1843.

POSTMASTER GENERAL—FRANCIS GRANGER, of New York, continued from preceding administration. SELAH R. HOBBIE, of New York (First Assistant Postmaster General), ad interim, September, 14, 1841. CHARLES A. WICKLIFFE, of Kentucky, September 13, 1841; entered upon duties October 13, 1841.

SECRETARY OF THE NAVY—GEORGE E. BADGER, of North Carolina, continued from preceding administration. JOHN D. SIMMS (chief clerk), ad interim, September 11, 1841. ABEL P. UPSHUR, of Virginia, September 13, 1841; entered upon duties

October 11, 1841. DAVID HENSHAW, of Massachusetts, July 24, 1843. THOMAS W. GILMER, of Virginia, February 15, 1844; entered upon duties February 19, 1844 (killed by the explosion of a gun on the U. S. S. *Princeton* February 28, 1844). LEWIS WARRINGTON (captain, United States Navy), ad interim, February 29, 1844. JOHN Y. MASON, of Virginia, March 14, 1844; entered upon duties March 20, 1844.

Administration of JAMES K. POLK

MARCH 4, 1845, TO MARCH 3, 1849

PRESIDENT OF THE UNITED STATES—JAMES K. POLK, of Tennessee.
VICE PRESIDENT OF THE UNITED STATES—GEORGE M. DALLAS, of Pennsylvania.
SECRETARY OF STATE—JOHN C. CALHOUN, of South Carolina, continued from preceding administration. JAMES BUCHANAN, of Pennsylvania, March 6, 1845; entered upon duties March 10, 1845.
SECRETARY OF THE TREASURY—GEORGE M. BIBB, of Kentucky, continued from preceding administration. ROBERT J. WALKER, of Mississippi, March 6, 1845; entered upon duties March 8, 1845.
SECRETARY OF WAR—WILLIAM WILKINS, of Pennsylvania, continued from preceding administration. WILLIAM L. MARCY, of New York, March 6, 1845; entered upon duties March 8, 1845.
ATTORNEY GENERAL—JOHN NELSON, of Maryland, continued from preceding administration. JOHN Y. MASON, of Virginia, March 6, 1845; entered upon duties March 11, 1845. NATHAN CLIFFORD, of Maine, October 17, 1846, to March 18, 1848, when he resigned. ISAAC TOUCEY, of Connecticut, June 21, 1848; entered upon duties June 29, 1848.
POSTMASTER GENERAL—CHARLES A. WICKLIFFE, of Kentucky, continued from preceding administration. CAVE JOHNSON, of Tennessee, March 6, 1845.
SECRETARY OF THE NAVY—JOHN Y. MASON, of Virginia, continued from preceding administration. GEORGE BANCROFT, of Massachusetts, March 10, 1845. JOHN Y. MASON, of Virginia, September 9, 1846.

Administration of ZACHARY TAYLOR

MARCH 4, 1849, TO JULY 9, 1850

PRESIDENT OF THE UNITED STATES—ZACHARY TAYLOR, of Louisiana. (Oath administered March 5, 1849. Died July 9, 1850.)
VICE PRESIDENT OF THE UNITED STATES—MILLARD FILLMORE, of New York.
SECRETARY OF STATE—JAMES BUCHANAN, of Pennsylvania, continued from preceding administration. JOHN M. CLAYTON, of Delaware, March 7, 1849.
SECRETARY OF THE TREASURY—ROBERT J. WALKER, of Mississippi, continued from preceding administration. McCLINTOCK YOUNG (chief clerk), ad interim, March 6, 1849. WILLIAM M. MEREDITH, of Pennsylvania, March 8, 1849.
SECRETARY OF WAR—WILLIAM L. MARCY, of New York, continued from preceding administration. REVERDY JOHNSON, of Maryland (Attorney General), ad interim, March 8, 1849. GEORGE W. CRAWFORD, of Georgia, March 8, 1849; entered upon duties March 14, 1849.
ATTORNEY GENERAL—ISAAC TOUCEY, of Connecticut, continued from preceding administration. REVERDY JOHNSON, of Maryland, March 8, 1849.
POSTMASTER GENERAL—CAVE JOHNSON, of Tennessee, continued from preceding administration. SELAH R. HOBBIE, of New York (First Assistant Postmaster General), ad interim, March 6, 1849. JACOB COLLAMER, of Vermont, March 8, 1849.
SECRETARY OF THE NAVY—JOHN Y. MASON, of Virginia, continued from preceding administration. WILLIAM B. PRESTON, of Virginia, March 8, 1849.
SECRETARY OF THE INTERIOR—THOMAS EWING, of Ohio, March 8, 1849.

Administration of MILLARD FILLMORE

JULY 10, 1850, TO MARCH 3, 1853

PRESIDENT OF THE UNITED STATES—MILLARD FILLMORE, of New York.
PRESIDENT PRO TEMPORE OF THE SENATE—WILLIAM R. KING, of Alabama; DAVID R. ATCHISON, of Missouri.

SECRETARY OF STATE—JOHN M. CLAYTON, of Delaware, continued from preceding administration. DANIEL WEBSTER, of Massachusetts, July 22, 1850 (died October 24, 1852). CHARLES M. CONRAD, of Louisiana (Secretary of War), ad interim, October 25, 1852. EDWARD EVERETT, of Massachusetts, November 6, 1852.

SECRETARY OF THE TREASURY—WILLIAM M. MEREDITH, of Pennsylvania, continued from preceding administration. THOMAS CORWIN, of Ohio, July 23, 1850.

SECRETARY OF WAR—GEORGE W. CRAWFORD, of Georgia, continued from preceding administration. SAMUEL J. ANDERSON (chief clerk), ad interim, July 23, 1850. WINFIELD SCOTT (major general, U. S. Army), ad interim, July 24, 1850. CHARLES M. CONRAD, of Louisiana, August 15, 1850.

ATTORNEY GENERAL—REVERDY JOHNSON, of Maryland, continued from preceding administration, served to July 22, 1850. JOHN J. CRITTENDEN, of Kentucky, July 22, 1850; entered upon duties August 14, 1850.

POSTMASTER GENERAL—JACOB COLLAMER, of Vermont, continued from preceding administration. NATHAN K. HALL, of New York, July 23, 1850. SAMUEL D. HUBBARD, of Connecticut, August 31, 1852; entered upon duties September 14, 1852.

SECRETARY OF THE NAVY—WILLIAM B. PRESTON, of Virginia, continued from preceding administration. LEWIS WARRINGTON (captain, U. S. Navy), ad interim, July 23, 1850. WILLIAM A. GRAHAM, of North Carolina, July 22, 1850; entered upon duties August 2, 1850. JOHN P. KENNEDY, of Maryland, July 22, 1852; entered upon duties July 26, 1852.

SECRETARY OF THE INTERIOR—THOMAS EWING, of Ohio continued from preceding administration. DANIEL C. GODDARD (chief clerk), ad interim, July 23, 1850. THOMAS M. T. MCKENNAN, of Pennsylvania, August 15, 1850. DANIEL C. GODDARD (chief clerk), ad interim, August 27, 1850. ALEXANDER H. H. STUART, of Virginia, September 12, 1850; entered upon duties September 16, 1850.

———

Administration of FRANKLIN PIERCE

MARCH 4, 1853, TO MARCH 3, 1857

PRESIDENT OF THE UNITED STATES—FRANKLIN PIERCE, of New Hampshire.

VICE PRESIDENT OF THE UNITED STATES—WILLIAM R. KING, of Alabama. (Died April 18, 1853.)

PRESIDENT PRO TEMPORE OF THE SENATE—DAVID R. ATCHISON, of Missouri; LEWIS CASS, of Michigan; JESSE D. BRIGHT, of Indiana; CHARLES E. STUART, of Michigan; JAMES M. MASON, of Virginia.

SECRETARY OF STATE—WILLIAM HUNTER (chief clerk), ad interim, March 4, 1853. WILLIAM L. MARCY, of New York, March 7, 1853.

SECRETARY OF THE TREASURY—THOMAS CORWIN, of Ohio, continued from preceding administration. JAMES GUTHRIE, of Kentucky, March 7, 1853.

SECRETARY OF WAR—CHARLES M. CONRAD, of Louisiana, continued from preceding administration. JEFFERSON DAVIS, of Mississippi, March 7, 1853. SAMUEL COOPER (Adjutant General, U. S. Army), ad interim, March 3, 1857.

ATTORNEY GENERAL—JOHN J. CRITTENDEN, of Kentucky, continued from preceding administration. CALEB CUSHING, of Massachusetts, March 7, 1853.

POSTMASTER GENERAL—SAMUEL D. HUBBARD, of Connecticut, continued from preceding administration. JAMES CAMPBELL, of Pennsylvania, March 7, 1853.

SECRETARY OF THE NAVY—JOHN P. KENNEDY, of Maryland, continued from preceding admihistration. JAMES C. DOBBIN, of North Carolina, March 7, 1853.

SECRETARY OF THE INTERIOR—ALEXANDER H. H. STUART, of Virginia, continued from preceding administration. ROBERT MCCLELLAND, of Michigan, March 7, 1853.

———

Administration of JAMES BUCHANAN

MARCH 4, 1857, TO MARCH 3, 1861

PRESIDENT OF THE UNITED STATES—JAMES BUCHANAN, of Pennsylvania.

VICE PRESIDENT OF THE UNITED STATES—JOHN C. BRECKINRIDGE, of Kentucky.

SECRETARY OF STATE—WILLIAM L. MARCY, of New York, continued from preceding administration. LEWIS CASS, of Michigan, March 6, 1857. WILLIAM HUNTER (chief clerk), ad interim, December 15, 1860. JEREMIAH S. BLACK, of Pennsylvania, December 17, 1860.

SECRETARY OF THE TREASURY—JAMES GUTHRIE, of Kentucky, continued from preceding administration. HOWELL COBB, of Georgia, March 6, 1857. ISAAC TOUCEY, of Connecticut (Secretary of the Navy), ad interim, December 10, 1860. PHILIP F. THOMAS, of Maryland, December 12, 1860. JOHN A. DIX, of New York, January 11, 1861; entered upon duties January 15, 1861.

SECRETARY OF WAR—SAMUEL COOPER (Adjutant General, U. S. Army), ad interim, March 4, 1857. JOHN B. FLOYD, of Virginia, March 6, 1857. JOSEPH HOLT, of Kentucky (Postmaster General), ad interim, January 1, 1861. JOSEPH HOLT, of Kentucky, January 18, 1861.

ATTORNEY GENERAL—CALEB CUSHING, of Massachusetts, continued from preceding administration. JEREMIAH S. BLACK, of Pennsylvania, March 6, 1857; entered upon duties March 11, 1857. EDWIN M. STANTON, of Pennsylvania, December 20, 1860; entered upon duties December 22, 1860.

POSTMASTER GENERAL—JAMES CAMPBELL, of Pennsylvania, continued from preceding administration. AARON V. BROWN, of Tennessee, March 6, 1857 (died March 8, 1859). HORATIO KING, of Maine (First Assistant Postmaster General), ad interim, March 9, 1859. JOSEPH HOLT, of Kentucky, March 14, 1859. HORATIO KING, of Maine (First Assistant Postmaster General), ad interim, January 1, 1861. HORATIO KING, of Maine, February 12, 1861.

SECRETARY OF THE NAVY—JAMES C. DOBBIN, of North Carolina, continued from preceding administration. ISAAC TOUCEY, of Connecticut, March 6, 1857.

SECRETARY OF THE INTERIOR—ROBERT McCLELLAND, of Michigan, continued from preceding administration. JACOB THOMPSON, of Mississippi, March 6, 1857; entered upon duties March 10, 1857. MOSES KELLY (chief clerk), ad interim, January 10, 1861.

First Administration of ABRAHAM LINCOLN

MARCH 4, 1861, TO MARCH 3, 1865

PRESIDENT OF THE UNITED STATES—ABRAHAM LINCOLN, of Illinois.
VICE PRESIDENT OF THE UNITED STATES—HANNIBAL HAMLIN, of Maine.
SECRETARY OF STATE—JEREMIAH S. BLACK, of Pennsylvania, continued from preceding administration. WILLIAM H. SEWARD, of New York, March 5, 1861.
SECRETARY OF THE TREASURY—JOHN A. DIX, of New York, continued from preceding administration. SALMON P. CHASE, of Ohio, March 5, 1861; entered upon duties March 7, 1861. GEORGE HARRINGTON, of the District of Columbia (Assistant Secretary), ad interim, July 1, 1864. WILLIAM P. FESSENDEN, of Maine, July 1, 1864; entered upon duties July 5, 1864.
SECRETARY OF WAR—JOSEPH HOLT, of Kentucky, continued from preceding administration. SIMON CAMERON, of Pennsylvania, March 5, 1861; entered upon duties March 11, 1861. EDWIN M. STANTON, of Pennsylvania, January 15, 1862; entered upon duties January 20, 1862.
ATTORNEY GENERAL—EDWIN M. STANTON, of Pennsylvania, continued from preceding administration. EDWARD BATES, of Missouri, March 5, 1861. JAMES SPEED, of Kentucky, December 2, 1864; entered upon duties December 5, 1864.
POSTMASTER GENERAL—HORATIO KING, of Maine, continued from preceding administration. MONTGOMERY BLAIR, of the District of Columbia, March 5, 1861; entered upon duties March 9, 1861. WILLIAM DENNISON, of Ohio, September 24, 1864; entered upon duties October 1, 1864.
SECRETARY OF THE NAVY—ISAAC TOUCEY, of Connecticut, continued from preceding administration. GIDEON WELLES, of Connecticut, March 5, 1861; entered upon duties March 7, 1861.
SECRETARY OF THE INTERIOR—MOSES KELLY (chief clerk), ad interim, March 4, 1861. CALEB B. SMITH, of Indiana, March 5, 1861. JOHN P. USHER, of Indiana (Assistant Secretary), ad interim, January 1, 1863. JOHN P. USHER, of Indiana, January 8, 1863.

Second Administration of ABRAHAM LINCOLN

MARCH 4, 1865, TO APRIL 15. 1865

PRESIDENT OF THE UNITED STATES—ABRAHAM LINCOLN, of Illinois. (Died April 15, 1865.)

VICE PRESIDENT OF THE UNITED STATES—ANDREW JOHNSON, of Tennessee.

SECRETARY OF STATE—WILLIAM H. SEWARD, of New York, continued from preceding administration.

SECRETARY OF THE TREASURY—GEORGE HARRINGTON, of the District of Columbia (Assistant Secretary), ad interim, March 4, 1865. HUGH MCCULLOCH, of Indiana, March 7, 1865; entered upon duties March 9, 1865.

SECRETARY OF WAR—EDWIN M. STANTON, of Pennsylvania, continued from preceding administration.

ATTORNEY GENERAL—JAMES SPEED, of Kentucky, continued from preceding administration.

POSTMASTER GENERAL—WILLIAM DENNISON, of Ohio, continued from preceding administration.

SECRETARY OF THE NAVY—GIDEON WELLES, of Connecticut, continued from preceding administration.

SECRETARY OF THE INTERIOR—JOHN P. USHER, of Indiana, continued from preceding administration.

Administration of ANDREW JOHNSON

APRIL 15, 1865, TO MARCH 3, 1869

PRESIDENT OF THE UNITED STATES—ANDREW JOHNSON, of Tennessee.

PRESIDENT PRO TEMPORE OF THE SENATE—LAFAYETTE S. FOSTER, of Connecticut; BENJAMIN F. WADE, of Ohio.

SECRETARY OF STATE—WILLIAM H. SEWARD, of New York, continued from preceding administration.

SECRETARY OF THE TREASURY—HUGH MCCULLOCH, of Indiana, continued from preceding administration.

SECRETARY OF WAR—EDWIN M. STANTON, of Pennsylvania, continued from preceding administration; suspended August 12, 1867. ULYSSES S. GRANT (General of the Army), ad interim, August 12, 1867. EDWIN M. STANTON, of Pennsylvania, reinstated January 13, 1868, to May 26, 1868. JOHN M. SCHOFIELD, of Illinois, May 28, 1868; entered upon duties June 1, 1868.

ATTORNEY GENERAL—JAMES SPEED, of Kentucky, continued from preceding administration. J. HUBLEY ASHTON, of Pennsylvania (Assistant Attorney General), acting, July 17, 1866. HENRY STANBERY, of Ohio, July 23, 1866. ORVILLE H. BROWNING, of Illinois (Secretary of the Interior), ad interim, March 13, 1868. WILLIAM M. EVARTS, of New York, July 15, 1868; entered upon duties July 20, 1868.

POSTMASTER GENERAL—WILLIAM DENNISON, of Ohio, continued from preceding administration. ALEXANDER W. RANDALL, of Wisconsin (First Assistant Postmaster General), ad interim, July 17, 1866. ALEXANDER W. RANDALL, of Wisconsin, July 25, 1866.

SECRETARY OF THE NAVY—GIDEON WELLES, of Connecticut, continued from preceding administration.

SECRETARY OF THE INTERIOR—JOHN P. USHER, of Indiana, continued from preceding administration. JAMES HARLAN, of Iowa, May 15, 1865. ORVILLE H. BROWNING, of Illinois, July 27, 1866, to take effect September 1, 1866.

First Administration of ULYSSES S. GRANT

MARCH 4, 1869, TO MARCH 3, 1873

PRESIDENT OF THE UNITED STATES—ULYSSES S. GRANT, of Illinois.

VICE PRESIDENT OF THE UNITED STATES—SCHUYLER COLFAX, of Indiana.

SECRETARY OF STATE—WILLIAM H. SEWARD, of New York, continued from preceding administration. ELIHU B. WASHBURNE, of Illinois, March 5, 1869. HAMILTON FISH, of New York, March 11, 1869; entered upon duties March 17, 1869.

SECRETARY OF THE TREASURY—HUGH MCCULLOCH, of Indiana, continued from preceding administration. JOHN F. HARTLEY, of Maine (Assistant Secretary), ad interim, March 5, 1869. GEORGE S. BOUTWELL, of Massachusetts, March 11, 1869.

SECRETARY OF WAR—JOHN M. SCHOFIELD, of Illinois, continued from preceding administration. JOHN A. RAWLINS, of Illinois, March 11, 1869. WILLIAM T. SHERMAN, of Ohio, September 9, 1869; entered upon duties September 11, 1869. WILLIAM W. BELKNAP, of Iowa, October 25, 1869; entered upon duties November 1, 1869.

ATTORNEY GENERAL—WILLIAM M. EVARTS, of New York, continued from preceding administration. J. HUBLEY ASHTON, of Pennsylvania (Assistant Attorney General), acting, March 5, 1869. EBENEZER R. HOAR, of Massachusetts, March 5,

1869; entered upon duties March 11, 1869. Amos T. Akerman, of Georgia, June 23, 1870; entered upon duties July 8, 1870. George H. Williams, of Oregon, December 14, 1871, to take effect January 10, 1872.

POSTMASTER GENERAL—St. John B. L. Skinner, of New York (First Assistant Postmaster General), ad interim, March 4, 1869. John A. J. Creswell, of Maryland, March 5, 1869.

SECRETARY OF THE NAVY—William Faxon, of Connecticut (Assistant Secretary), ad interim, March 4, 1869. Adolph E. Borie, of Pennsylvania, March 5, 1869; entered upon duties March 9, 1869. George M. Robeson, of New Jersey, June 25, 1869.

SECRETARY OF THE INTERIOR—William T. Otto, of Indiana (Assistant Secretary), ad interim, March 4, 1869. Jacob D. Cox, of Ohio, March 5, 1869; entered upon duties March 9, 1869. Columbus Delano, of Ohio, November 1, 1870.

Second Administration of ULYSSES S. GRANT

MARCH 4, 1873, TO MARCH 3, 1877

PRESIDENT OF THE UNITED STATES—Ulysses S. Grant, of Illinois.

VICE PRESIDENT OF THE UNITED STATES—Henry Wilson, of Massachusetts. (Died November 22, 1875.)

PRESIDENT PRO TEMPORE OF THE SENATE—Thomas W. Ferry, of Michigan.

SECRETARY OF STATE—Hamilton Fish, of New York, continued from preceding administration. Hamilton Fish, of New York, recommissioned March 17, 1873.

SECRETARY OF THE TREASURY—George S. Boutwell, of Massachusetts, continued from preceding administration. William A. Richardson, of Massachusetts, March 17, 1873. Benjamin H. Bristow, of Kentucky, June 2, 1874; entered upon duties June 4, 1874. Charles F. Conant, of New Hampshire (Assistant Secretary), ad interim, June 21, 1876, to June 30, 1876. Lot M. Morrill, of Maine, June 21, 1876; entered upon duties July 7, 1876.

SECRETARY OF WAR—William W. Belknap, of Iowa, continued from preceding administration. William W. Belknap, of Iowa, recommissioned March 17, 1873. George M. Robeson, of New Jersey (Secretary of the Navy), ad interim, March 2, 1876. Alphonso Taft, of Ohio, March 8, 1876; entered upon duties March 11, 1876. James D. Cameron, of Pennsylvania, May 22, 1876; entered upon duties June 1, 1876.

ATTORNEY GENERAL—George H. Williams, of Oregon, continued from preceding administration. George H. Williams, of Oregon, recommissioned March 17, 1873. Edwards Pierrepont, of New York, April 26, 1875, to take effect May 15, 1875. Alphonso Taft, of Ohio, May 22, 1876; entered upon duties June 1, 1876.

POSTMASTER GENERAL—John A. J. Creswell, of Maryland, continued from preceding administration. John A. J. Creswell, of Maryland, recommissioned March 17, 1873. James W. Marshall, of Virginia, July 3, 1874; entered upon duties July 7, 1874. Marshall Jewell, of Connecticut, August 24, 1874; entered upon duties September 1, 1874. James N. Tyner, of Indiana, July 12, 1876.

SECRETARY OF THE NAVY—George M. Robeson, of New Jersey, continued from preceding administration. George M. Robeson, of New Jersey, recommissioned March 17, 1873.

SECRETARY OF THE INTERIOR—Columbus Delano, of Ohio, continued from preceding administration. Columbus Delano, of Ohio, recommissioned March 17, 1873. Benjamin R. Cowen, of Ohio (Assistant Secretary), ad interim, October 1, 1875. Zachariah Chandler, of Michigan, October 19, 1875.

Administration of RUTHERFORD B. HAYES

MARCH 4, 1877, TO MARCH 3, 1881

PRESIDENT OF THE UNITED STATES—Rutherford B. Hayes, of Ohio. (Oath administered March 5, 1877.)

VICE PRESIDENT OF THE UNITED STATES—William A. Wheeler, of New York.

SECRETARY OF STATE—Hamilton Fish, of New York, continued from preceding administration. William M. Evarts, of New York, March 12, 1877.

SECRETARY OF THE TREASURY—Lot M. Morrill, of Maine, continued from preceding administration. John Sherman, of Ohio, March 8, 1877; entered upon duties March 10, 1877.

SECRETARY OF WAR—James D. Cameron, of Pennsylvania, continued from preceding administration. George W. McCrary, of Iowa, March 12, 1877. Alexander Ramsey, of Minnesota, December 10, 1879; entered upon duties December 12, 1879.

ATTORNEY GENERAL—Alphonso Taft, of Ohio, continued from preceding administration. Charles Devens, of Massachusetts, March 12, 1877.

POSTMASTER GENERAL—James N. Tyner, of Indiana, continued from preceding administration. David M. Key, of Tennessee, March 12, 1877; resigned June 1, 1880; served to August 24, 1880. Horace Maynard, of Tennessee, June 2, 1880; entered upon duties August 25, 1880.

SECRETARY OF THE NAVY—George M. Robeson, of New Jersey, continued from preceding administration. Richard W. Thompson, of Indiana, March 12, 1877. Alexander Ramsey, of Minnesota (Secretary of War), ad interim, December 20, 1880. Nathan Goff, Jr., of West Virginia, January 6, 1881.

SECRETARY OF THE INTERIOR—Zachariah Chandler, of Michigan, continued from preceding administration. Carl Schurz, of Missouri, March 12, 1877.

———

Administration of JAMES A. GARFIELD

MARCH 4, 1881, TO SEPTEMBER 19, 1881

PRESIDENT OF THE UNITED STATES—James A. Garfield, of Ohio. (Died September 19, 1881.)

VICE PRESIDENT OF THE UNITED STATES—Chester A. Arthur, of New York.

SECRETARY OF STATE—William M. Evarts, of New York, continued from preceding administration. James G. Blaine, of Maine, March 5, 1881; entered upon duties March 7, 1881.

SECRETARY OF THE TREASURY—Henry F. French, of Massachusetts (Assistant Secretary), ad interim, March 4, 1881. William Windom, of Minnesota, March 5, 1881; entered upon duties March 8, 1881.

SECRETARY OF WAR—Alexander Ramsey, of Minnesota, continued from preceding administration. Robert T. Lincoln, of Illinois, March 5, 1881; entered upon duties March 11, 1881.

ATTORNEY GENERAL—Charles Devens, of Massachusetts, continued from preceding administration. Wayne MacVeagh, of Pennsylvania, March 5, 1881; entered upon duties March 7, 1881.

POSTMASTER GENERAL—Horace Maynard, of Tennessee, continued from preceding administration. Thomas L. James, of New York, March 5, 1881; entered upon duties March 8, 1881.

SECRETARY OF THE NAVY—Nathan Goff, Jr., of West Virginia, continued from preceding administration. William H. Hunt, of Louisiana, March 5, 1881; entered upon duties March 7, 1881.

SECRETARY OF THE INTERIOR—Carl Schurz, of Missouri, continued from preceding administration. Samuel J. Kirkwood, of Iowa, March 5, 1881; entered upon duties March 8, 1881.

———

Administration of CHESTER A. ARTHUR

SEPTEMBER 20, 1881, TO MARCH 3, 1885

PRESIDENT OF THE UNITED STATES—Chester A. Arthur, of New York.

PRESIDENT PRO TEMPORE OF THE SENATE—Thomas F. Bayard, of Delaware; David Davis, of Illinois; George F. Edmunds, of Vermont.

SECRETARY OF STATE—James G. Blaine, of Maine, continued from preceding administration. Frederick T. Frelinghuysen, of New Jersey, December 12, 1881; entered upon duties December 19, 1881.

SECRETARY OF THE TREASURY—WILLIAM WINDOM, of Minnesota, continued from preceding administration. CHARLES J. FOLGER, of New York, October 27, 1881; entered upon duties November 14, 1881 (died September 4, 1884). CHARLES E. COON, of New York (Assistant Secretary), ad interim, September 4, 1884. HENRY F. FRENCH, of Massachusetts (Assistant Secretary), ad interim, September 8, 1884. CHARLES E. COON, of New York (Assistant Secretary), ad interim, September 15, 1884. WALTER Q. GRESHAM, of Indiana, September 24, 1884. HENRY F. FRENCH, of Massachusetts (Assistant Secretary), ad interim, October 29, 1884. HUGH MCCULLOCH, of Indiana, October 28, 1884; entered upon duties October 31, 1884.

SECRETARY OF WAR—ROBERT T. LINCOLN, of Illinois, continued from preceding administration.

ATTORNEY GENERAL—WAYNE MACVEAGH, of Pennsylvania, continued from preceding administration. SAMUEL F. PHILLIPS, of North Carolina (Solicitor General), ad interim, November 14, 1881. BENJAMIN H. BREWSTER, of Pennsylvania, December 19, 1881; entered upon duties January 3, 1882.

POSTMASTER GENERAL—THOMAS L. JAMES, of New York, continued from preceding administration. THOMAS L. JAMES, of New York, recommissioned October 27, 1881. TIMOTHY O. HOWE, of Wisconsin, December 20, 1881; entered upon duties January 5, 1882 (died March 25, 1883). FRANK HATTON, of Iowa (First Assistant Postmaster General), ad interim, March 26, 1883. WALTER Q. GRESHAM, of Indiana, April 3, 1883; entered upon duties April 11, 1883. FRANK HATTON, of Iowa (First Assistant Postmaster General), ad interim, September 25, 1884. FRANK HATTON, of Iowa, October 14, 1884.

SECRETARY OF THE NAVY—WILLIAM H. HUNT, of Louisiana, continued from preceding administration. WILLIAM E. CHANDLER, of New Hampshire, April 12, 1882; entered upon duties April 17, 1882.

SECRETARY OF THE INTERIOR—SAMUEL J. KIRKWOOD, of Iowa, continued from preceding administration. HENRY M. TELLER, of Colorado, April 6, 1882; entered upon duties April 17, 1882.

First Administration of GROVER CLEVELAND

MARCH 4, 1885, TO MARCH 3, 1889

PRESIDENT OF THE UNITED STATES—GROVER CLEVELAND, of New York.

VICE PRESIDENT OF THE UNITED STATES—THOMAS A. HENDRICKS, of Indiana, (Died November 25, 1885.)

PRESIDENT PRO TEMPORE OF THE SENATE—JOHN SHERMAN, of Ohio; JOHN J. INGALLS, of Kansas.

SECRETARY OF STATE—FREDERICK T. FRELINGHUYSEN, of New Jersey, continued from preceding administration. THOMAS F. BAYARD, of Delaware, March 6, 1885.

SECRETARY OF THE TREASURY—HUGH MCCULLOCH, of Indiana, continued from preceding administration. DANIEL MANNING, of New York, March 6, 1885; entered upon duties March 8, 1885. CHARLES S. FAIRCHILD, of New York, April 1, 1887.

SECRETARY OF WAR—ROBERT T. LINCOLN, of Illinois, continued from preceding administration. WILLIAM C. ENDICOTT, of Massachusetts, March 6, 1885.

ATTORNEY GENERAL—BENJAMIN H. BREWSTER, of Pennsylvania, continued from preceding administration. AUGUSTUS H. GARLAND, of Arkansas, March 6, 1885; entered upon duties March 9, 1885.

POSTMASTER GENERAL—FRANK HATTON, of Iowa, continued from preceding administration. WILLIAM F. VILAS, of Wisconsin, March 6, 1885. DON M. DICKINSON, of Michigan, January 16, 1888.

SECRETARY OF THE NAVY—WILLIAM E. CHANDLER, of New Hampshire, continued from preceding administration. WILLIAM C. WHITNEY, of New York, March 6, 1885.

SECRETARY OF THE INTERIOR—MERRITT L. JOSLYN, of Illinois (Assistant Secretary), ad interim, March 4, 1885. LUCIUS Q. C. LAMAR, of Mississippi, March 6, 1885. HENRY L. MULDROW, of Mississippi (First Assistant Secretary), ad interim, January 11, 1888. WILLIAM F. VILAS, of Wisconsin, January 16, 1888.

SECRETARY OF AGRICULTURE—NORMAN J. COLMAN, of Missouri, February 13, 1889.

Administration of BENJAMIN HARRISON

MARCH 4, 1889, TO MARCH 3, 1893

PRESIDENT OF THE UNITED STATES—BENJAMIN HARRISON, of Indiana.

VICE PRESIDENT OF THE UNITED STATES—LEVI P. MORTON, of New York.

SECRETARY OF STATE—THOMAS F. BAYARD, of Delaware, continued from preceding administration. JAMES G. BLAINE, of Maine, March 5, 1889; entered upon duties March 7, 1889. WILLIAM F. WHARTON, of Massachusetts (Assistant Secretary), ad interim, June 4, 1892. JOHN W. FOSTER, of Indiana, June 29, 1892. WILLIAM F. WHARTON, of Massachusetts (Assistant Secretary), ad interim, February 23, 1893.

SECRETARY OF THE TREASURY—CHARLES S. FAIRCHILD, of New York, continued from preceding administration. WILLIAM WINDOM, of Minnesota, March 5, 1889; entered upon duties March 7, 1889 (ed January 29, 1891). ALLURED B. NETTLETON, of Minnesota (Assistant Secretary), ad interim, January 30, 1891. CHARLES FOSTER, of Ohio, February 24, 1891.

SECRETARY OF WAR—WILLIAM C. ENDICOTT, of Massachusetts, continued from preceding administration. REDFIELD PROCTOR, of Vermont, March 5, 1889. LEWIS A. GRANT, of Minnesota (Assistant Secretary), ad interim, December 6, 1891. STEPHEN B. ELKINS, of West Virginia, December 22, 1891; entered upon duties December 24, 1891.

ATTORNEY GENERAL—AUGUSTUS H. GARLAND, of Arkansas, continued from preceding administration. WILLIAM H. H. MILLER, of Indiana, March 5, 1889.

POSTMASTER GENERAL—DON M. DICKINSON, of Michigan, continued from preceding administration. JOHN WANAMAKER, of Pennsylvania, March 5, 1889.

SECRETARY OF THE NAVY—WILLIAM C. WHITNEY, of New York, continued from preceding administration. BENJAMIN F. TRACY, of New York, March 5, 1889.

SECRETARY OF THE INTERIOR—WILLIAM F. VILAS, of Wisconsin, continued from preceding administration. JOHN W. NOBLE, of Missouri, March 5, 1889; entered upon duties March 7, 1889.

SECRETARY OF AGRICULTURE—NORMAN J. COLMAN, of Missouri, continued from preceding administration. JEREMIAH M. RUSK, of Wisconsin, March 5, 1889; entered upon duties March 7, 1889.

Second Administration of GROVER CLEVELAND

MARCH 4, 1893, TO MARCH 3, 1897

PRESIDENT OF THE UNITED STATES—GROVER CLEVELAND, of New York.

VICE PRESIDENT OF THE UNITED STATES—ADLAI E. STEVENSON, of Illinois.

SECRETARY OF STATE—WILLIAM F. WHARTON, of Massachusetts (Assistant Secretary), ad interim, continued from preceding administration. WALTER Q. GRESHAM, of Illinois, March 6, 1893 (died May 28, 1895). EDWIN F. UHL, of Michigan (Assistant Secretary), ad interim, May 28, 1895. ALVEY A. ADEE, of the District of Columbia (Second Assistant Secretary), ad interim, May 31, 1895. EDWIN F. UHL, of Michigan (Assistant Secretary), ad interim, June 1, 1895. RICHARD OLNEY, of Massachusetts, June 8, 1895; entered upon duties June 10, 1895.

SECRETARY OF THE TREASURY—CHARLES FOSTER, of Ohio, continued from preceding administration. JOHN G. CARLISLE, of Kentucky, March 6, 1893.

SECRETARY OF WAR—STEPHEN B. ELKINS, of West Virginia, continued from preceding administration. DANIEL S. LAMONT, of New York, March 6, 1893.

ATTORNEY GENERAL—WILLIAM H. H. MILLER, of Indiana, continued from preceding administration. RICHARD OLNEY, of Massachusetts, March 6, 1893. JUDSON HARMON, of Ohio, June 8, 1895; entered upon duties June 11, 1895.

POSTMASTER GENERAL—JOHN WANAMAKER, of Pennsylvania, continued from preceding administration. WILSON S. BISSELL, of New York, March 6, 1893. WILLIAM L. WILSON, of West Virginia, March 1, 1895; entered upon duties April 4, 1895.

SECRETARY OF THE NAVY—BENJAMIN F. TRACY, of New York, continued from preceding administration. HILARY A. HERBERT, of Alabama, March 6, 1893.

SECRETARY OF THE INTERIOR—JOHN W. NOBLE, of Missouri, continued from preceding administration. HOKE SMITH, of Georgia, March 6, 1893. JOHN M. REYNOLDS, of Pennsylvania (Assistant Secretary), ad interim, September 1, 1896. DAVID R. FRANCIS, of Missouri, September 1, 1896; entered upon duties September 4, 1896.

SECRETARY OF AGRICULTURE—JEREMIAH M. RUSK, of Wisconsin, continued from preceding administration. JULIUS STERLING MORTON, of Nebraska, March 6, 1893.

First Administration of WILLIAM McKINLEY

MARCH 4, 1897, TO MARCH 3, 1901

PRESIDENT OF THE UNITED STATES—WILLIAM McKINLEY, of Ohio.

VICE PRESIDENT OF THE UNITED STATES—GARRET A. HOBART, of New Jersey. (Died November 21, 1899.)

PRESIDENT PRO TEMPORE OF THE SENATE—WILLIAM P. FRYE, of Maine.

SECRETARY OF STATE—RICHARD OLNEY, of Massachusetts, continued from preceding administration. JOHN SHERMAN, of Ohio, March 5, 1897; WILLIAM R. DAY, of Ohio, April 26, 1898; entered upon duties April 28, 1898. ALVEY A. ADEE (Second Assistant Secretary), ad interim, September 17, 1898. JOHN HAY, of the District of Columbia, September 20, 1898; entered upon duties September 30, 1898.

SECRETARY OF THE TREASURY—JOHN G. CARLISLE, of Kentucky, continued from preceding administration. LYMAN J. GAGE, of Illinois, March 5, 1897.

SECRETARY OF WAR—DANIEL S. LAMONT, of New York, continued from preceding administration. RUSSELL A. ALGER, of Michigan, March 5, 1897. ELIHU ROOT, of New York, August 1, 1899.

ATTORNEY GENERAL—JUDSON HARMON, of Ohio, continued from preceding administration. JOSEPH McKENNA, of California, March 5, 1897; entered upon duties March 7, 1897. JOHN K. RICHARDS, of Ohio (Solicitor General), ad interim, January 26, 1898; JOHN W. GRIGGS, of New Jersey, January 25, 1898; entered upon duties February 1, 1898.

POSTMASTER GENERAL—WILLIAM L. WILSON, of West Virginia, continued from preceding administration. JAMES A. GARY, of Maryland, March 5, 1897. CHARLES EMORY SMITH, of Pennsylvania, April 21, 1898.

SECRETARY OF THE NAVY—HILARY A. HERBERT, of Alabama, continued from preceding administration. JOHN D. LONG, of Massachusetts, March 5, 1897.

SECRETARY OF THE INTERIOR—DAVID R. FRANCIS, of Missouri, continued from preceding administration. CORNELIUS N. BLISS, of New York, March 5, 1897. ETHAN A. HITCHCOCK, of Missouri, December 21, 1898; entered upon duties February 20, 1899.

SECRETARY OF AGRICULTURE—JULIUS STERLING MORTON, of Nebraska, continued from preceding administration. JAMES WILSON, of Iowa, March 5, 1897.

Second Administration of WILLIAM McKINLEY

MARCH 4, 1901, TO SEPTEMBER 14, 1901

PRESIDENT OF THE UNITED STATES—WILLIAM McKINLEY, of Ohio. (Died September 14, 1901.)

VICE PRESIDENT OF THE UNITED STATES—THEODORE ROOSEVELT, of New York.

SECRETARY OF STATE—JOHN HAY, of the District of Columbia, continued from preceding administration. JOHN HAY, of the District of Columbia, recommissioned March 5, 1901.

SECRETARY OF THE TREASURY—LYMAN J. GAGE, of Illinois, continued from preceding administration. LYMAN J. GAGE, of Illinois, recommissioned March 5, 1901.

SECRETARY OF WAR—ELIHU ROOT, of New York, continued from preceding administration. ELIHU ROOT, of New York, recommissioned March 5, 1901.

ATTORNEY GENERAL—JOHN W. GRIGGS, of New Jersey, continued from preceding administration. JOHN W. GRIGGS, of New Jersey, recommissioned March 5, 1901. JOHN K. RICHARDS, of Ohio (Solicitor General), ad interim, April 1, 1901. PHILANDER C. KNOX, of Pennsylvania, April 5, 1901; entered upon duties April 10, 1901.

POSTMASTER GENERAL—CHARLES EMORY SMITH, of Pennsylvania, continued from preceding administration. CHARLES EMORY SMITH, of Pennsylvania, recommissioned March 5, 1901.

SECRETARY OF THE NAVY—JOHN D. LONG, of Massachusetts, continued from preceding administration. JOHN D. LONG, of Massachusetts, recommissioned March 5, 1901.

SECRETARY OF THE INTERIOR—Ethan A. Hitchcock, of Missouri, continued from preceding administration. Ethan A. Hitchcock, of Missouri, recommissioned March 5, 1901.

SECRETARY OF AGRICULTURE—James Wilson, of Iowa, continued from preceding administration. James Wilson, of Iowa, recommissioned March 5, 1901.

First Administration of THEODORE ROOSEVELT

SEPTEMBER 14, 1901, TO MARCH 3, 1905

PRESIDENT OF THE UNITED STATES—Theodore Roosevelt, of New York.

PRESIDENT PRO TEMPORE OF THE SENATE—William P. Frye, of Maine.

SECRETARY OF STATE—John Hay, of the District of Columbia, continued from preceding administration.

SECRETARY OF THE TREASURY—Lyman J. Gage, of Illinois, continued from preceding administration. Leslie M. Shaw, of Iowa, January 9, 1902; entered upon duties February 1, 1902.

SECRETARY OF WAR—Elihu Root, of New York, continued from preceding administration. William H. Taft, of Ohio, January 11, 1904, to take effect February 1, 1904.

ATTORNEY GENERAL—Philander C. Knox, of Pennsylvania, continued from preceding administration. Philander C. Knox, of Pennsylvania, recommissioned December 16, 1901. William H. Moody, of Massachusetts, July 1, 1904.

POSTMASTER GENERAL—Charles Emory Smith, of Pennsylvania, continued from preceding administration. Henry C. Payne, of Wisconsin, January 9, 1902. Robert J. Wynne, of Pennsylvania, October 10, 1904.

SECRETARY OF THE NAVY—John D. Long, of Massachusetts, continued from preceding administration. William H. Moody, of Massachusetts, April 29, 1902; entered upon duties May 1, 1902. Paul Morton, of Illinois, July 1, 1904.

SECRETARY OF THE INTERIOR—Ethan A. Hitchcock, of Missouri, continued from preceding administration.

SECRETARY OF AGRICULTURE—James Wilson, of Iowa, continued from preceding administration.

SECRETARY OF COMMERCE AND LABOR—George B. Cortelyou, of New York, February 16, 1903. Victor H. Metcalf, of California, July 1, 1904.

Second Administration of THEODORE ROOSEVELT

MARCH 4, 1905, TO MARCH 3, 1909

PRESIDENT OF THE UNITED STATES—Theodore Roosevelt, of New York.

VICE PRESIDENT OF THE UNITED STATES—Charles Warren Fairbanks, of Indiana.

SECRETARY OF STATE—John Hay, of the District of Columbia, continued from preceding administration. John Hay, of the District of Columbia, recommissioned March 6, 1905 (died July 1, 1905). Francis B. Loomis, of Ohio (Assistant Secretary), ad interim, July 1, 1905, to July 18, 1905. Elihu Root, of New York, July 7, 1905, entered upon duties July 19, 1905. Robert Bacon, of New York, January 27, 1909.

SECRETARY OF THE TREASURY—Leslie M. Shaw, of Iowa, continued from preceding administration. Leslie M. Shaw, of Iowa, recommissioned March 6, 1905. George B. Cortelyou, of New York, January 15, 1907, to take effect March 4, 1907.

SECRETARY OF WAR—William H. Taft, of Ohio, continued from preceding administration. William H. Taft, of Ohio, recommissioned March 6, 1905. Luke E. Wright, of Tennessee, June 29, 1908; entered upon duties July 1, 1908.

ATTORNEY GENERAL—WILLIAM H. MOODY, of Massachusetts, continued from preceding administration. WILLIAM H. MOODY, of Massachusetts, recommissioned March 6, 1905. CHARLES J. BONAPARTE, of Maryland, December 12, 1906; entered upon duties December 17, 1906.

POSTMASTER GENERAL—ROBERT J. WYNNE, of Pennsylvania, continued from preceding administration. GEORGE B. CORTELYOU, of New York, March 6, 1905. GEORGE VON L. MEYER, of Massachusetts, January 15, 1907, to take effect March 4, 1907.

SECRETARY OF THE NAVY—PAUL MORTON, of Illinois, continued from preceding administration. PAUL MORTON, of Illinois, recommissioned March 6, 1905. CHARLES J. BONAPARTE, of Maryland, July 1, 1905. VICTOR H. METCALF, of California, December 12, 1906; entered upon duties December 17, 1906. TRUMAN H. NEWBERRY, of Michigan, December 1, 1908.

SECRETARY OF THE INTERIOR—ETHAN A. HITCHCOCK, of Missouri, continued from preceding administration. ETHAN A. HITCHCOCK, of Missouri, recommissioned March 6, 1905. JAMES R. GARFIELD, of Ohio, January 15, 1907, to take effect March 4, 1907.

SECRETARY OF AGRICULTURE—JAMES WILSON, of Iowa, continued from preceding administration. JAMES WILSON, of Iowa, recommissioned March 6, 1905.

SECRETARY OF COMMERCE AND LABOR—VICTOR H. METCALF, of California, continued from preceding administration. VICTOR H. METCALF, of California, recommissioned March 6, 1905. OSCAR S. STRAUS, of New York, December 12, 1906; entered upon duties December 17, 1906.

Administration of WILLIAM H. TAFT

MARCH 4, 1909, TO MARCH 3, 1913

PRESIDENT OF THE UNITED STATES—WILLIAM H. TAFT, of Ohio.

VICE PRESIDENT OF THE UNITED STATES—JAMES S. SHERMAN, of New York. (Died October 30, 1912.)

PRESIDENT PRO TEMPORE OF THE SENATE—WILLIAM P. FRYE, of Maine (resigned April 27, 1911). JACOB H. GALLINGER, of New Hampshire, and AUGUSTUS O. BACON, of Georgia, alternating.

SECRETARY OF STATE—ROBERT BACON, of New York, continued from preceding administration. PHILANDER C. KNOX, of Pennsylvania, March 5, 1909.

SECRETARY OF THE TREASURY—GEORGE B. CORTELYOU, of New York, continued from preceding administration. FRANKLIN MACVEAGH, of Illinois, March 5, 1909; entered upon duties March 8, 1909.

SECRETARY OF WAR—LUKE E. WRIGHT, of Tennessee, continued from preceding administration. JACOB M. DICKINSON, of Tennessee, March 5, 1909; entered upon duties March 12, 1909. HENRY L. STIMSON, of New York, May 16, 1911; entered upon duties May 22, 1911.

ATTORNEY GENERAL—CHARLES J. BONAPARTE, of Maryland, continued from preceding administration. GEORGE W. WICKERSHAM, of New York, March 5, 1909.

POSTMASTER GENERAL—GEORGE VON L. MEYER, of Massachusetts, continued from preceding administration. FRANK H. HITCHCOCK, of Massachusetts, March 5, 1909.

SECRETARY OF THE NAVY—TRUMAN H. NEWBERRY, of Michigan, continued from preceding administration. GEORGE VON L. MEYER, of Massachusetts, March 5, 1909.

SECRETARY OF THE INTERIOR—JAMES R. GARFIELD, of Ohio, continued from preceding administration. RICHARD A. BALLINGER, of Washington, March 5, 1909. WALTER LOWRIE FISHER, of Illinois, March 7, 1911.

SECRETARY OF AGRICULTURE—JAMES WILSON, of Iowa, continued from preceding administration. JAMES WILSON, of Iowa, recommissioned March 5, 1909.

SECRETARY OF COMMERCE AND LABOR—OSCAR S. STRAUS, of New York, continued from preceding administration. CHARLES NAGEL, of Missouri, March 5, 1909.

First Administration of WOODROW WILSON

MARCH 4, 1913, TO MARCH 3, 1917

PRESIDENT OF THE UNITED STATES—WOODROW WILSON, of New Jersey.

VICE PRESIDENT OF THE UNITED STATES—THOMAS R. MARSHALL, of Indiana.

SECRETARY OF STATE—PHILANDER C. KNOX, of Pennsylvania, continued from preceding administration. WILLIAM JENNINGS BRYAN, of Nebraska, March 5, 1913. ROBERT LANSING, of New York (counselor), ad interim, June 9, 1915. ROBERT LANSING, of New York, June 23, 1915.

SECRETARY OF THE TREASURY—FRANKLIN MACVEAGH, of Illinois, continued from preceding administration. WILLIAM GIBBS MCADOO, of New York, March 5, 1913; entered upon duties March 6, 1913.

SECRETARY OF WAR—HENRY L. STIMSON, of New York, continued from preceding administration. LINDLEY M. GARRISON, of New Jersey, March 5, 1913. HUGH L. SCOTT (United States Army), ad interim, February 12, 1916; served from February 11 to March 8, 1916. NEWTON D. BAKER, of Ohio, March 7, 1916; entered upon duties March 9, 1916.

ATTORNEY GENERAL—GEORGE W. WICKERSHAM, of New York, continued from preceding administration. JAMES CLARK MCREYNOLDS, of Tennessee, March 5, 1913; entered upon duties March 6, 1913. THOMAS WATT GREGORY, of Texas, August 29, 1914; entered upon duties September 3, 1914.

POSTMASTER GENERAL—FRANK H. HITCHCOCK, of Massachusetts, continued from preceding administration. ALBERT SIDNEY BURLESON, of Texas, March 5, 1913.

SECRETARY OF THE NAVY—GEORGE VON L. MEYER, of Massachusetts, continued from preceding administration. JOSEPHUS DANIELS, of North Carolina, March 5, 1913.

SECRETARY OF THE INTERIOR—WALTER LOWRIE FISHER, of Illinois, continued from preceding administration. FRANKLIN KNIGHT LANE, of California, March 5, 1913.

SECRETARY OF AGRICULTURE—JAMES WILSON, of Iowa, continued from preceding administration. DAVID FRANKLIN HOUSTON, of Missouri, March 5, 1913; entered upon duties March 6, 1913.

SECRETARY OF COMMERCE—CHARLES NAGEL, of Missouri (Secretary of Commerce and Labor), continued from preceding administration. WILLIAM C. REDFIELD, of New York, March 5, 1913.

SECRETARY OF LABOR—CHARLES NAGEL, of Missouri (Secretary of Commerce and Labor), continued from preceding administration. WILLIAM BAUCHOP WILSON, of Pennsylvania, March 5, 1913.

Second Administration of WOODROW WILSON

MARCH 4, 1917, TO MARCH 3, 1921

PRESIDENT OF THE UNITED STATES—WOODROW WILSON, of New Jersey. (Oath administered March 5, 1917.)

VICE PRESIDENT OF THE UNITED STATES—THOMAS R. MARSHALL, of Indiana.

SECRETARY OF STATE—ROBERT LANSING, of New York, continued from preceding administration. FRANK L. POLK, of New York (Undersecretary), ad interim, February 14, 1920, to March 13, 1920. BAINBRIDGE COLBY, of New York, March 22, 1920; entered upon duties March 23, 1920.

SECRETARY OF THE TREASURY—WILLIAM GIBBS MCADOO, of New York, continued from preceding administration. CARTER GLASS, of Virginia, December 6, 1918; entered upon duties December 16, 1918. DAVID F. HOUSTON, of Missouri, January 31, 1920; entered upon duties February 2, 1920.

SECRETARY OF WAR—NEWTON D. BAKER, of Ohio, continued from preceding administration.

ATTORNEY GENERAL—THOMAS WATT GREGORY, of Texas, continued from preceding administration. A. MITCHELL PALMER, of Pennsylvania, March 5, 1919.

POSTMASTER GENERAL—ALBERT SIDNEY BURLESON, of Texas, continued from preceding administration. ALBERT SIDNEY BURLESON, of Texas, recommissioned January 24, 1918.

SECRETARY OF THE NAVY—JOSEPHUS DANIELS, of North Carolina, continued from preceding administration.

SECRETARY OF THE INTERIOR—FRANKLIN KNIGHT LANE, of California, continued from preceding administration. JOHN BARTON PAYNE, of Illinois, February 28, 1920; entered upon duties March 13, 1920.

SECRETARY OF AGRICULTURE—DAVID FRANKLIN HOUSTON, of Missouri, continued from preceding administration. EDWIN T. MEREDITH, of Iowa, January 31, 1920; entered upon duties February 2, 1920.

SECRETARY OF COMMERCE—WILLIAM C. REDFIELD, of New York, continued from preceding administration. JOSHUA WILLIS ALEXANDER, of Missouri, December 11, 1919; entered upon duties December 16, 1919.

SECRETARY OF LABOR—WILLIAM BAUCHOP WILSON, of Pennsylvania, continued from preceding administration.

Administration of WARREN G. HARDING

MARCH 4, 1921, TO AUGUST 2, 1923

PRESIDENT OF THE UNITED STATES—WARREN G. HARDING, of Ohio. (Died August 2, 1923.)

VICE PRESIDENT OF THE UNITED STATES—CALVIN COOLIDGE, of Massachusetts.

SECRETARY OF STATE—BAINBRIDGE COLBY, of New York, continued from preceding administration. CHARLES EVANS HUGHES, of New York, March 4, 1921; entered upon duties March 5, 1921.

SECRETARY OF THE TREASURY—DAVID F. HOUSTON, of Missouri, continued from preceding administration. ANDREW W. MELLON, of Pennsylvania, March 4, 1921; entered upon duties March 5, 1921.

SECRETARY OF WAR—NEWTON D. BAKER, of Ohio, continued from preceding administration. JOHN W. WEEKS, of Massachusetts, March 5, 1921.

ATTORNEY GENERAL—A. MITCHELL PALMER, of Pennsylvania, continued from preceding administration. HARRY M. DAUGHERTY, of Ohio, March 5, 1921.

POSTMASTER GENERAL—ALBERT SIDNEY BURLESON, of Texas, continued from preceding administration. WILL H. HAYS, of Indiana, March 5, 1921. HUBERT WORK, of Colorado, March 4, 1922. HARRY S. NEW, of Indiana, February 27, 1923; entered upon duties March 5, 1923.

SECRETARY OF THE NAVY—JOSEPHUS DANIELS, of North Carolina, continued from preceding administration. EDWIN DENBY, of Michigan, March 5, 1921.

SECRETARY OF THE INTERIOR—JOHN BARTON PAYNE, of Illinois, continued from preceding administration. ALBERT B. FALL, of New Mexico, March 5, 1921. HUBERT WORK, of Colorado, February 27, 1923; entered upon duties March 5, 1923.

SECRETARY OF AGRICULTURE—EDWIN T. MEREDITH, of Iowa, continued from preceding administration. HENRY C. WALLACE, of Iowa, March 5, 1921.

SECRETARY OF COMMERCE—JOSHUA WILLIS ALEXANDER, of Missouri, continued from preceding administration. HERBERT C. HOOVER, of California, March 5, 1921.

SECRETARY OF LABOR—WILLIAM BAUCHOP·WILSON, of Pennsylvania, continued from preceding administration. JAMES J. DAVIS, of Pennsylvania, March 5, 1921.

First Administration of CALVIN COOLIDGE

AUGUST 3, 1923, TO MARCH 3, 1925

PRESIDENT OF THE UNITED STATES—CALVIN COOLIDGE, of Massachusetts.

PRESIDENT PRO TEMPORE OF THE SENATE—ALBERT B. CUMMINS, of Iowa.

SECRETARY OF STATE—CHARLES EVANS HUGHES, of New York, continued from preceding administration.

SECRETARY OF THE TREASURY—ANDREW W. MELLON, of Pennsylvania, continued from preceding administration.

SECRETARY OF WAR—JOHN W. WEEKS, of Massachusetts, continued from preceding administration.

ATTORNEY GENERAL—HARRY M. DAUGHERTY, of Ohio, continued from preceding administration. HARLAN F. STONE, of New York, April 7, 1924; entered upon duties April 9, 1924.

POSTMASTER GENERAL—HARRY S. NEW, of Indiana, continued from preceding administration.

SECRETARY OF THE NAVY—EDWIN DENBY, of Michigan, continued from preceding administration. CURTIS D. WILBUR, of California, March 18, 1924.

SECRETARY OF THE INTERIOR—HUBERT WORK, of Colorado, continued from preceding administration.

SECRETARY OF AGRICULTURE—HENRY C. WALLACE, of Iowa, continued from preceding administration (died October 25, 1924). HOWARD M. GORE, of West Virginia (Assistant Secretary), ad interim, October 26, 1924, to November 22, 1924. HOWARD M. GORE, of West Virginia, November 21, 1924; entered upon duties November 22, 1924.

SECRETARY OF COMMERCE—HERBERT C. HOOVER, of California, continued from preceding administration.

SECRETARY OF LABOR—JAMES J. DAVIS, of Pennsylvania, continued from preceding administration.

Second Administration of CALVIN COOLIDGE

MARCH 4, 1925, TO MARCH 3, 1929

PRESIDENT OF THE UNITED STATES—CALVIN COOLIDGE, of Massachusetts.

VICE PRESIDENT OF THE UNITED STATES—CHARLES G. DAWES, of Illinois.

SECRETARY OF STATE—CHARLES EVANS HUGHES, of New York, continued from preceding administration. FRANK B. KELLOGG, of Minnesota, February 16, 1925; entered upon duties March 5, 1925.

SECRETARY OF THE TREASURY—ANDREW W. MELLON, of Pennsylvania, continued from preceding administration.

SECRETARY OF WAR—JOHN W. WEEKS, of Massachusetts, continued from preceding administration. DWIGHT F. DAVIS, of Missouri, October 13, 1925; entered upon duties October 14, 1925.

ATTORNEY GENERAL—JAMES M. BECK, of Pennsylvania (Solicitor General), ad interim, March 4, 1925, to March 16, 1925. JOHN G. SARGENT, of Vermont, March 17, 1925; entered upon duties March 18, 1925.

POSTMASTER GENERAL—HARRY S. NEW, of Indiana, continued from preceding administration. HARRY S. NEW, of Indiana, recommissioned March 5, 1925.

SECRETARY OF THE NAVY—CURTIS D. WILBUR, of California, continued from preceding administration.

SECRETARY OF THE INTERIOR—HUBERT WORK, of Colorado, continued from preceding administration. ROY O. WEST, of Illinois, ad interim, July 25, 1928, to January 21, 1929. ROY O. WEST, January 21, 1929.

SECRETARY OF AGRICULTURE—HOWARD M. GORE, of West Virginia, continued from preceding administration. WILLIAM M. JARDINE, of Kansas, February 18, 1925; entered upon duties March 5, 1925.

SECRETARY OF COMMERCE—HERBERT C. HOOVER, of California, continued from preceding administration. WILLIAM F. WHITING, of Massachusetts, ad interim, August 21, 1928, to December 11, 1928. WILLIAM F. WHITING, December 11, 1928.

SECRETARY OF LABOR—JAMES J. DAVIS, of Pennsylvania, continued from preceding administration.

Administration of HERBERT C. HOOVER

MARCH 4, 1929, TO MARCH 3, 1933

PRESIDENT OF THE UNITED STATES—HERBERT C. HOOVER, of California.

VICE PRESIDENT OF THE UNITED STATES—CHARLES CURTIS, of Kansas.

SECRETARY OF STATE—FRANK B. KELLOGG, of Minnesota, continued from preceding administration. HENRY L. STIMSON, of New York, March 4, 1929; entered upon duties March 29, 1929.

SECRETARY OF THE TREASURY—ANDREW W. MELLON, of Pennsylvania, continued from preceding administration. OGDEN L. MILLS, of New York, February 10, 1932; entered upon duties February 13, 1932.

SECRETARY OF WAR—DWIGHT F. DAVIS, of Missouri, continued from preceding administration. JAMES W. GOOD, of Illinois, March 5, 1929; entered upon duties March 6, 1929. PATRICK J. HURLEY, of Oklahoma, December 9, 1929.

ATTORNEY GENERAL—JOHN G. SARGENT, of Vermont, continued from preceding administration. JAMES DEWITT MITCHELL, of Minnesota, March 5, 1929; entered upon duties March 6, 1929.

POSTMASTER GENERAL—HARRY S. NEW, of Indiana, continued from preceding administration. WALTER F. BROWN, of Ohio, March 5, 1929; entered upon duties March 6, 1929.

SECRETARY OF THE NAVY—CURTIS D. WILBUR, of California, continued from preceding administration. CHARLES F. ADAMS, of Massachusetts, March 5, 1929.

SECRETARY OF THE INTERIOR—ROY O. WEST, of Illinois, continued from preceding administration. RAY L. WILBUR, of California, March 5, 1929.

SECRETARY OF AGRICULTURE—WILLIAM M. JARDINE, of Kansas, continued from preceding administration, ARTHUR M. HYDE, of Missouri, March 5, 1929; entered upon duties March 6, 1929.

SECRETARY OF COMMERCE—WILLIAM F. WHITING, of Massachusetts, continued from preceding administration. ROBERT P. LAMONT, of Illinois, March 5, 1929. ROY D. CHAPIN, of Michigan, ad interim, August 8, 1932, to December 14, 1932. ROY D. CHAPIN, of Michigan, December 14, 1932.

SECRETARY OF LABOR—James J. Davis, of Pennsylyania, continued from preceding administration. William N. Doak, of Virginia, December 8, 1930; entered upon duties December 9, 1930.

First Administration of FRANKLIN DELANO ROOSEVELT

MARCH 4, 1933, TO JANUARY 20, 1937

PRESIDENT OF THE UNITED STATES—Franklin Delano Roosevelt, of New York.

VICE PRESIDENT OF THE UNITED STATES—John N. Garner, of Texas.

SECRETARY OF STATE—Cordell Hull, of Tennessee, March 4, 1933.

SECRETARY OF THE TREASURY—William H. Woodin, of New York, March 4, 1933. Henry Morgenthau, Jr., of New York (Under Secretary), ad interim, January 1, 1934, to January 8, 1934. Henry Morgenthau, Jr., of New York, January 8, 1934.

SECRETARY OF WAR—George H. Dern, of Utah, March 4, 1933.

ATTORNEY GENERAL—Homer S. Cummings, of Connecticut, March 4, 1933.

POSTMASTER GENERAL—James A. Farley, of New York, March 4, 1933.

SECRETARY OF THE NAVY—Claude A. Swanson, of Virginia, March 4, 1933.

SECRETARY OF THE INTERIOR—Harold L. Ickes, of Illinois, March 4, 1933.

SECRETARY OF AGRICULTURE—Henry A. Wallace, of Iowa, March 4, 1933.

SECRETARY OF COMMERCE—Daniel C. Roper, of South Carolina, March 4, 1933.

SECRETARY OF LABOR—Frances Perkins, of New York, March 4, 1933.

Second Administration of FRANKLIN DELANO ROOSEVELT

JANUARY 20, 1937, TO JANUARY 20, 1941

PRESIDENT OF THE UNITED STATES—Franklin Delano Roosevelt, of New York.

VICE PRESIDENT OF THE UNITED STATES—John N. Garner, of Texas.

SECRETARY OF STATE—Cordell Hull, of Tennessee, continued from preceding administration.

SECRETARY OF THE TREASURY—Henry Morgenthau, Jr., of New York, continued from preceding administration.

SECRETARY OF WAR—George H. Dern, of Utah, continued from preceding administration (died August 27, 1936). Harry H. Woodring, of Kansas (Assistant Secretary), ad interim, September 25, 1936, to May 6, 1937. Harry H. Woodring, of Kansas, May 6, 1937. Henry L. Stimson, of New York, July 10, 1940.

ATTORNEY GENERAL—Homer S. Cummings, of Connecticut, continued from preceding administration. Frank Murphy, of Michigan, ad interim, January 2, 1939, to January 17, 1939. Frank Murphy, of Michigan, January 17, 1939. Robert H. Jackson, of New York, January 18, 1940.

POSTMASTER GENERAL—James A. Farley, of New York, continued from preceding administration. James A. Farley, of New York, recommissioned January 22, 1937. Frank C. Walker, of Pennsylvania, September 10, 1940.

SECRETARY OF THE NAVY—Claude A. Swanson, of Virginia, continued from preceding administration (died July 7, 1939). Charles Edison, of New Jersey, Acting Secretary from August 5, 1939, to December 30, 1939. Charles Edison, of New Jersey (Assistant Secretary), ad interim, December 30, 1939, to January 11, 1940. Charles Edison, of New Jersey, January 11, 1940. Frank Knox, of Illinois, July 10, 1940.

SECRETARY OF THE INTERIOR—Harold L. Ickes, of Illinois, continued from preceding administration.

SECRETARY OF AGRICULTURE—Henry A. Wallace, of Iowa, continued from preceding administration Claude R. Wickard, of Indiana, August 27, 1940; entered upon duties September 5, 1940.

SECRETARY OF COMMERCE—Daniel C. Roper, of South Carolina, continued from preceding administration. Harry L. Hopkins, of New York, ad interim, December 24, 1938, to January 23, 1939. Harry L..Hopkins, of New York, January 23, 1939. Jesse H. Jones, of Texas, September 16, 1940; entered upon duties September 19, 1940.

SECRETARY OF LABOR—Frances Perkins, of New York, continued from preceding administration.

Third Administration of FRANKLIN DELANO ROOSEVELT

JANUARY 20, 1941, TO JANUARY 20, 1945

PRESIDENT OF THE UNITED STATES—Franklin Delano Roosevelt, of New York.

VICE PRESIDENT OF THE UNITED STATES—Henry A. Wallace, of Iowa.

SECRETARY OF STATE—Cordell Hull, of Tennessee, continued from preceding administration. Edward R. Stettinius, of Virginia, November 30, 1944; entered upon duties December 1, 1944.

SECRETARY OF THE TREASURY—Henry Morgenthau, Jr., of New York, continued from preceding administration.

SECRETARY OF WAR—Henry L. Stimson, of New York, continued from preceding administration.

ATTORNEY GENERAL—Robert H. Jackson, of New York, continued from preceding administration. Francis Biddle, of Pennsylvania, September 5, 1941.

POSTMASTER GENERAL—Frank C. Walker, of Pennsylvania, continued from preceding administration. Frank C. Walker, of Pennsylvania, recommissioned January 27, 1941.

SECRETARY OF THE NAVY—Frank Knox, of Illinois, continued from preceding administration (died April 28, 1944). James V. Forrestal, of New York, May 18, 1944.

SECRETARY OF THE INTERIOR—Harold L. Ickes, of Illinois, continued from preceding administration.

SECRETARY OF AGRICULTURE—Claude R. Wickard, of Indiana, continued from preceding administration.

SECRETARY OF COMMERCE—Jesse H. Jones, of Texas, continued from preceding administration.

SECRETARY OF LABOR—Frances Perkins, of New York, continued from preceding administration.

Fourth Administration of FRANKLIN DELANO ROOSEVELT

JANUARY 20, 1945, TO APRIL 12, 1945

PRESIDENT OF THE UNITED STATES—Franklin Delano Roosevelt, of New York. (Died April 12, 1945.)

VICE PRESIDENT OF THE UNITED STATES—Harry S. Truman, of Missouri.

SECRETARY OF STATE—Edward R. Stettinius, of Virginia, continued from preceding administration.

SECRETARY OF THE TREASURY—Henry Morgenthau, Jr., of New York, continued from preceding administration.

SECRETARY OF WAR—Henry L. Stimson, of New York, continued from preceding administration.

ATTORNEY GENERAL—Francis Biddle, of Pennsylvania, continued from preceding administration.

POSTMASTER GENERAL—Frank C. Walker, of Pennsylvania, continued from preceding administration. Frank C. Walker, of Pennsylvania, recommissioned February 6, 1945.

SECRETARY OF THE NAVY—James V. Forrestal, of New York, continued from preceding administration.

SECRETARY OF THE INTERIOR—Harold L. Ickes, of Illinois, continued from preceding administration.

SECRETARY OF AGRICULTURE—Claude R. Wickard, of Indiana, continued from preceding administration.

SECRETARY OF COMMERCE—Jesse H. Jones, of Texas, continued from preceding administration. Henry A. Wallace, of Iowa, March 1, 1945; entered upon duties March 2, 1945.

SECRETARY OF LABOR—Frances Perkins, of New York, continued from preceding administration.

First Administration of HARRY S. TRUMAN

APRIL 12, 1945, TO JANUARY 20, 1949

PRESIDENT OF THE UNITED STATES—HARRY S. TRUMAN, of Missouri.

PRESIDENT PRO TEMPORE OF THE SENATE—KENNETH MCKELLAR, of Tennessee. ARTHUR S. VANDENBERG, of Michigan, January 4, 1947.

SECRETARY OF STATE—EDWARD R. STETTINIUS, of Virginia, continued from preceding administration. JAMES F. BYRNES, of South Carolina, July 2, 1945; entered upon duties July 3, 1945. GEORGE C. MARSHALL, of Pennsylvania, January 8, 1947; entered upon duties January 21, 1947.

SECRETARY OF THE TREASURY—HENRY MORGENTHAU, JR., of New York, continued from preceding administration. FRED M. VINSON, of Kentucky, July 18, 1945; entered upon duties July 23, 1945. JOHN W. SNYDER, of Missouri, June 12, 1946; entered upon duties June 25, 1946.

SECRETARY OF DEFENSE—JAMES FORRESTAL, of New York, July 26, 1947; entered upon duties September 17, 1947.

SECRETARY OF WAR—HENRY L. STIMSON, of New York, continued from preceding administration. ROBERT PORTER PATTERSON, of New York, September 26, 1945; entered upon duties September 27, 1945. KENNETH C. ROYALL, of North Carolina, July 21, 1947; entered upon duties July 25, 1947, and served until September 17, 1947.

ATTORNEY GENERAL—FRANCIS BIDDLE, of Pennsylvania, continued from preceding administration. TOM C. CLARK, of Texas, June 15, 1945; entered upon duties July 1, 1945.

POSTMASTER GENERAL—FRANK C. WALKER, of Pennsylvania, continued from preceding administration. ROBERT E. HANNEGAN, of Missouri, May 8, 1945; entered upon duties July 1, 1945. JESSE M. DONALDSON, of Missouri, December 16, 1947.

SECRETARY OF THE NAVY—JAMES V. FORRESTAL, of New York, continued from preceding administration; served until September 17, 1947.

SECRETARY OF THE INTERIOR—HAROLD L. ICKES, of Illinois, continued from preceding administration. JULIUS A. KRUG, of Wisconsin, March 6, 1946; entered upon duties March 18, 1946.

SECRETARY OF AGRICULTURE—CLAUDE R. WICKARD, of Indiana, continued from preceding administration. CLINTON P. ANDERSON, of New Mexico, June 2, 1945; entered upon duties June 30, 1945. CHARLES F. BRANNAN, of Colorado, May 29, 1948; entered upon duties June 2, 1948.

SECRETARY OF COMMERCE—HENRY A. WALLACE, of Iowa, continued from preceding administration. WILLIAM AVERELL HARRIMAN, of New York, ad interim, September 28, 1946, to January 28, 1947. WILLIAM AVERELL HARRIMAN, of New York, January 28, 1947. CHARLES SAWYER, of Ohio, May 6, 1948.

SECRETARY OF LABOR—FRANCES PERKINS, of New York, continued from preceding administration. LEWIS B. SCHWELLENBACH, of Washington, June 1, 1945; entered upon duties July 1, 1945. (Died June 10, 1948.) MAURICE J. TOBIN, of Massachusetts, ad interim, August 13, 1948.

Second Administration of HARRY S. TRUMAN

JANUARY 20, 1949, TO JANUARY 20, 1953

PRESIDENT OF THE UNITED STATES—HARRY S. TRUMAN, of Missouri.

VICE PRESIDENT OF THE UNITED STATES—ALBEN W. BARKLEY, of Kentucky.

SECRETARY OF STATE—DEAN G. ACHESON, of Connecticut, January 19, 1949; entered upon duties January 21, 1949.

SECRETARY OF THE TREASURY—JOHN W. SNYDER, of Missouri, continued from preceding administration.

SECRETARY OF DEFENSE—JAMES FORRESTAL, of New York, continued from preceding administration. LOUIS A. JOHNSON, of West Virginia, March 23, 1949; entered upon duties March 28, 1949. GEORGE C. MARSHALL, of Pennsylvania, September 20, 1950; entered upon duties September 21, 1950. ROBERT A. LOVETT, of New York, September 14, 1951; entered upon duties September 17, 1951.

ATTORNEY GENERAL—TOM C. CLARK, of Texas, continued from preceding administration. J. HOWARD MCGRATH, of Rhode Island, August 19, 1949; entered upon duties August 24, 1949. JAMES P. MCGRANERY, of Pennsylvania, May 21, 1952; entered upon duties May 27, 1952.

POSTMASTER GENERAL—JESSE M. DONALDSON, of Missouri, continued from preceding administration. JESSE M. DONALDSON, of Missouri, recommissioned February 8, 1949.

SECRETARY OF THE INTERIOR—Julius A. Krug, of Wisconsin, continued from preceding administration. Oscar L. Chapman, of Colorado (Under Secretary), ad interim, December 1, 1949, to January 19, 1950. Oscar L. Chapman, of Colorado, January 19, 1950.

SECRETARY OF AGRICULTURE—Charles F. Brannan, of Colorado, continued from preceding administration.

SECRETARY OF COMMERCE—Charles Sawyer, of Ohio, continued from preceding administration.

SECRETARY OF LABOR—Maurice J. Tobin, of Massachusetts, ad interim, continued from preceding administration. Maurice J. Tobin, of Massachusetts, February 1, 1949.

First Administration of DWIGHT D. EISENHOWER

JANUARY 20, 1953, TO JANUARY 20, 1957

PRESIDENT OF THE UNITED STATES—Dwight D. Eisenhower, of New York.

VICE PRESIDENT OF THE UNITED STATES—Richard M. Nixon, of California.

SECRETARY OF STATE—John Foster Dulles, of New York, January 21, 1953.

SECRETARY OF THE TREASURY—George M. Humphrey, of Ohio, January 21, 1953.

SECRETARY OF DEFENSE—Charles E. Wilson, of Michigan, January 26, 1953; entered upon duties January 28, 1953.

ATTORNEY GENERAL—Herbert Brownell, Jr., of New York, January 21, 1953.

POSTMASTER GENERAL—Arthur E. Summerfield, of Michigan, January 21, 1953.

SECRETARY OF THE INTERIOR—Douglas McKay, of Oregon, January 21, 1953. Frederick A. Seaton, of Nebraska, June 6, 1956; entered upon duties June 8, 1956.

SECRETARY OF AGRICULTURE—Ezra Taft Benson, of Utah, January 21, 1953.

SECRETARY OF COMMERCE—Sinclair Weeks, of Massachusetts, January 21, 1953.

SECRETARY OF LABOR—Martin P. Durkin, of Maryland, January 21, 1953. James P. Mitchell, of New Jersey, ad interim, October 9, 1953, to January 19, 1954. James P. Mitchell, of New Jersey, January 19, 1954.

SECRETARY OF HEALTH, EDUCATION, AND WELFARE—Oveta Culp Hobby, of Texas, April 10, 1953; entered upon duties April 11, 1953. Marion B. Folsom, of New York, July 20, 1955; entered upon duties August 1, 1955.

Second Administration of DWIGHT D. EISENHOWER

JANUARY 20, 1957, TO JANUARY 20, 1961

PRESIDENT OF THE UNITED STATES—Dwight D. Eisenhower, of Pennsylvania.

VICE PRESIDENT OF THE UNITED STATES—Richard M. Nixon, of California.

SECRETARY OF STATE—John Foster Dulles, of New York, continued from preceding administration. Christian Herter, of Massachusetts, April 21, 1959; entered upon duties April 22, 1959.

SECRETARY OF THE TREASURY—George M. Humphrey, of Ohio, continued from preceding administration. Rose Bernerd Anderson, of Connecticut, July 2, 1957; entered upon duties July 29, 1957.

SECRETARY OF DEFENSE—Charles E. Wilson, of Michigan, continued from preceding administration. Neil H. McElroy, of Ohio, August 19, 1957; entered upon duties October 9, 1957. Thomas S. Gates, Jr., of Pennsylvania, ad interim, December 1, 1959, to January 26, 1960. Thomas S. Gates, Jr., of Pennsylvania, January 26, 1960.

ATTORNEY GENERAL—Herbert Brownell, Jr., of New York, continued from preceding administration. William Rogers, of Maryland, ad interim, November 8, 1957, to January 27, 1958. William P. Rogers, of Maryland, January 28, 1958.

POSTMASTER GENERAL—ARTHUR E. SUMMERFIELD, of Michigan, continued from preceding administration. ARTHUR SUMMERFIELD, of Michigan, recommissioned February 4, 1957.

SECRETARY OF THE INTERIOR—FREDERICK A. SEATON, of Nebraska, continued from preceding administration.

SECRETARY OF AGRICULTURE—EZRA TAFT BENSON, of Utah, continued from preceding administration.

SECRETARY OF COMMERCE—SINCLAIR WEEKS, of Massachusetts, continued from preceding administration. LEWIS STRAUSS, of New York, ad interim, November 13, 1958, to June 27, 1959. FREDERICK H. MUELLER, of Michigan Under Secretary), ad interim, July 21, 1959, to August 6, 1959. FREDERICK H. MUELLER, of Michigan, August 6, 1959.

SECRETARY OF LABOR—JAMES P. MITCHELL, of New Jersey, continued from preceding administration.

SECRETARY OF HEALTH, EDUCATION, AND WELFARE—MARION B. FOLSOM, of New York, continued from preceding administration. ARTHUR S. FLEMMING, of Ohio, July 9, 1958; entered upon duties August 1, 1958.

Administration of JOHN F. KENNEDY

JANUARY 20, 1961, TO NOVEMBER 22, 1963

PRESIDENT OF THE UNITED STATES—JOHN F. KENNEDY, of Massachusetts. (Died November 22, 1963.)

VICE PRESIDENT OF THE UNITED STATES—LYNDON B. JOHNSON, of Texas.

SECRETARY OF STATE—DEAN RUSK, of New York, January 21, 1961.

SECRETARY OF THE TREASURY—DOUGLAS DILLON, of New Jersey, January 21, 1961.

SECRETARY OF DEFENSE—ROBERT S. MCNAMARA, of Michigan, January 21, 1961.

ATTORNEY GENERAL—ROBERT F. KENNEDY, of Massachusetts, January 21, 1961.

POSTMASTER GENERAL—J. EDWARD DAY, of California, January 21, 1961. JOHN A. GRONOUSKI, of Wisconsin, September 24, 1963; entered upon duties September 30, 1963.

SECRETARY OF THE INTERIOR—STEWART L. UDALL, of Arizona, January 21, 1961.

SECRETARY OF AGRICULTURE—ORVILLE L. FREEMAN, of Minnesota, January 21, 1961.

SECRETARY OF COMMERCE—LUTHER H. HODGES, of North Carolina, January 21, 1961.

SECRETARY OF LABOR—ARTHUR J. GOLDBERG, of Illinois, January 21, 1961. W. WILLARD WIRTZ, of Illinois, September 24, 1962; entered upon duties September 25, 1962.

SECRETARY OF HEALTH, EDUCATION, AND WELFARE—ABRAHAM A. RIBICOFF, of Connecticut, January 21, 1962. ANTHONY J. CELEBREZZE, of Ohio, July 20, 1962; entered upon duties July 31, 1962.

First Administration of LYNDON B. JOHNSON

NOVEMBER 22, 1963, TO JANUARY 20, 1965

PRESIDENT OF THE UNITED STATES—LYNDON B. JOHNSON, of Texas.

SPEAKER OF THE HOUSE OF REPRESENTATIVES—JOHN W.MCCORMACK, of Massachusetts.

SECRETARY OF STATE—DEAN RUSK, of New York, continued from preceding administration.

SECRETARY OF THE TREASURY—DOUGLAS DILLON, of New Jersey, continued from preceding administration.

SECRETARY OF DEFENSE—ROBERT S. MCNAMARA, of Michigan, continued from preceding administration.

ATTORNEY GENERAL—ROBERT F. KENNEDY, of Massachusetts, continued from preceding administration. NICHOLAS DEB. KATZENBACH, of Illinois (Deputy Attorney General), ad interim, September 4, 1964.

POSTMASTER GENERAL—JOHN A. GRONOUSKI, of Wisconsin, continued from preceding administration.

SECRETARY OF THE INTERIOR—STEWART L. UDALL, of Arizona, continued from preceding administration.

SECRETARY OF AGRICULTURE—ORVILLE L. FREEMAN, of Minnesota, continued from preceding administration.

SECRETARY OF COMMERCE—LUTHER H. HODGES, of North Carolina, continued from preceding administration. JOHN T. O'CONNOR, of New Jersey, January 15, 1965; entered upon duties January 18, 1965.

SECRETARY OF LABOR—W. WILLARD WIRTZ, of Illinois, continued from preceding administration.

SECRETARY OF HEALTH, EDUCATION, AND WELFARE—ANTHONY J. CELEBREZZE, of Ohio, continued from preceding administration.

Second Administration of LYNDON B. JOHNSON

JANUARY 20, 1965, TO JANUARY 20, 1969

PRESIDENT OF THE UNITED STATES—LYNDON B. JOHNSON, of Texas.

VICE PRESIDENT OF THE UNITED STATES—HUBERT H. HUMPHREY, of Minnesota.

SECRETARY OF STATE—DEAN RUSK, of New York, continued from preceding administration.

SECRETARY OF THE TREASURY—DOUGLAS DILLON, of New Jersey, continued from preceding administration. HARRY H. FOWLER, of Virginia, March 25, 1965; entered upon duties April 1, 1965. JOSEPH W. BARR, of Indiana, entered upon duties December 21, 1968 (recess appointment); confirmed January 9, 1969.

SECRETARY OF DEFENSE—ROBERT S. MCNAMARA, of Michigan, continued from preceding administration. CLARK M. CLIFFORD, of Maryland, January 30, 1968; entered upon duties March 1, 1968.

ATTORNEY GENERAL—NICHOLAS DEB. KATZENBACH, of Illinois (Deputy Attorney General), ad interim, continued from preceding administration. NICHOLAS DEB. KATZENBACH, of Illinois, confirmed February 10, 1965; entered upon duties February 11, 1965. RAMSEY CLARK, of Texas, March 2, 1967.

POSTMASTER GENERAL—JOHN A. GRONOUSKI, of Wisconsin, continued from preceding administration. JOHN A. GRONOUSKI, of Wisconsin, recommissioned February 17, 1965. LAWRENCE F. O'BRIEN, of Massachusetts, September 1, 1965; entered upon duties November 3, 1965. W. MARVIN WATSON, of Texas, April 23, 1968; entered upon duties April 26, 1968.

SECRETARY OF THE INTERIOR—STEWART L. UDALL, of Arizona, continued from preceding administration.

SECRETARY OF AGRICULTURE—ORVILLE L. FREEMAN, of Minnesota, continued from preceding administration.

SECRETARY OF COMMERCE—JOHN T. O'CONNOR, of New Jersey, continued from preceding administration. ALEXANDER B. TROWBRIDGE, of New York, ad interim, February 1, 1967. ALEXANDER B. TROWBRIDGE, of New York, June 8, 1967; entered upon duties June 14, 1967. CYRUS R. SMITH, of New York, March 1, 1968; entered upon duties March 6, 1968.

SECRETARY OF LABOR—W. WILLARD WIRTZ, of Illinois, continued from preceding administration.

SECRETARY OF HEALTH, EDUCATION, AND WELFARE—ANTHONY J. CELEBREZZE, of Ohio, continued from preceding administration. JOHN W. GARDNER, of New York, August 11, 1965; entered upon duties August 18, 1965. WILBUR J. COHEN, of Michigan, ad interim, March 2, 1968. WILBUR J. COHEN, of Michigan, May 16, 1968.

SECRETARY OF HOUSING AND URBAN DEVELOPMENT—ROBERT C. WEAVER, of New York, January 17, 1966; entered upon duties January 18, 1966. ROBERT C. WOOD, of Florida, ad interim, January 2, 1969.

SECRETARY OF TRANSPORTATION—ALAN S. BOYD, of Florida, January 12, 1967; entered upon duties January 16, 1967.

Administration of RICHARD M. NIXON

JANUARY 20, 1969, to JANUARY 20, 1973

PRESIDENT OF THE UNITED STATES—RICHARD M. NIXON, of California.

VICE-PRESIDENT OF THE UNITED STATES—SPIRO T. AGNEW, of Maryland.

SECRETARY OF STATE—WILLIAM P. ROGERS, of New York and Maryland, January 1969.

SECRETARY OF THE TREASURY—DAVID M. KENNEDY, of Illinois, January 1969-January 1971. JOHN B. CONNALLY, of Texas, February 1971-May 1972. GEORGE P. SHULTZ, of New York, June 1972-March 1974.

SECRETARY OF DEFENSE—MELVIN R. LAIRD, of Wisconsin, January 1969-January 1973.

ATTORNEY-GENERAL—JOHN N. MITCHELL, of New York, January 1969-March 1972. RICHARD KLEINDIENST, of Arizona, June 1972-April 1973.

POSTMASTER GENERAL—WINTON M. BLOUNT, of Alabama, January 1969-July 1971.

SECRETARY OF THE INTERIOR—WALTER J. HICKEL, of Alaska, January 1969. FRED J. RUSSELL, of California, ad interim, November 1970. ROGERS C.B. MORTON, of Maryland, January 1971-March 1975.

SECRETARY OF AGRICULTURE—CLIFFORD M. HARDIN, of Missouri, January 1969-November 1971. EARL L. BUTZ, of Indiana, December 1971-October 1976.

SECRETARY OF COMMERCE—MAURICE H. STANS, of New York, January 1969-January 1972. PETER G. PETERSON, of Nebraska, February 1972-December 1972. FREDERICK B. DENT, of South Carolina, January 1973-March 1975.

SECRETARY OF LABOR—GEORGE P. SHULTZ, of New York, January 1969-July 1970. JAMES D. HODGSON, of California, July 1970-November 1972.

SECRETARY OF HEALTH, EDUCATION, AND WELFARE—ROBERT H. FINCH, of California, January 1969-June 1970. ELLIOT L. RICHARDSON, of Massachusetts, June 1970-January 1973.

SECRETARY OF HOUSING AND URBAN DEVELOPMENT—GEORGE ROMNEY, of Michigan, January 1969-November 1972.

SECRETARY OF TRANSPORTATION—JOHN A. VOLPE, of Massachusetts, January 1969-December 1972. CLAUDE S. BRINEGAR, of New York, January 1973-1975.

Administration of RICHARD M. NIXON

JANUARY 20, 1973, TO AUGUST 9, 1974

PRESIDENT OF THE UNITED STATES—Richard M. Nixon, of California.

VICE-PRESIDENT OF THE UNITED STATES—Spiro T. Agnew, of Maryland, January 1973-October 1973. Gerald R. Ford. of Michigan, December 1973-August 1974.

SECRETARY OF STATE—William P. Rogers, of New York and Maryland, January 1969-August 1973. Henry A. Kissinger, of Washington, D.C., September 1973-January 1977.

SECRETARY OF THE TREASURY—George P. Shultz, of New York, June 1972-March 1974. William E. Simon, of New Jersey, April 1974-January 1977.

SECRETARY OF DEFENSE—Melvin R. Laird, of Wisconsin, January 1969-January 1973. Elliot L. Richardson, of Massachusetts, January-May 1973. James R. Schlesinger, of Virginia, June 1973-November 1975.

ATTORNEY-GENERAL—Richard G. Kleindienst, of Arizona, June 1972-April 1973. Elliot L. Richardson, of Massachusetts, May, 1973-October 1973. William B. Saxbe, of Ohio, January 1974-December 1974.

SECRETARY OF THE INTERIOR—Rogers C.B. Morton, of Maryland, January 1971-March 1975.

SECRETARY OF AGRICULTURE—Earl L. Butz, of Indiana, December 1971-October 1976.

SECRETARY OF COMMERCE—Peter G. Peterson, of Nebraska, February-December 1972. Frederick B. Dent, of South Carolina, January 1973-March 1975.

SECRETARY OF LABOR—James D. Hodgson, of California, July 1970-November 1972. Peter J. Brennan, of New York, February 1973-February 1975.

SECRETARY OF HEALTH, EDUCATION AND WELFARE—Elliot L. Richardson, of Massachusetts, June 1970-January 1973. Caspar W. Weinberger, of California, February 1973-July 1975.

SECRETARY OF HOUSING AND URBAN DEVELOPMENT—James T. Lynn, of Ohio, February 1973-January 1975.

SECRETARY OF TRANSPORTATION—John A. Volpe, of Massachusetts, January 1969-December 1972. Claude S. Brinegar, of New York, January 1973-January 1975.

Administration of GERALD R. FORD

AUGUST 9, 1974, to JANUARY 20, 1977

PRESIDENT OF THE UNITED STATES—Gerald R. Ford, of Michigan.

VICE-PRESIDENT OF THE UNITED STATES—Nelson A. Rockefeller of New York, December 1974-January 1977.

SECRETARY OF STATE—Henry A. Kissinger, of Washington, D.C., September 1973-January 1977.

SECRETARY OF THE TREASURY—William E. Simon, of New Jersey, April 1974-January 1977.

SECRETARY OF DEFENSE—James R. Schlesinger, of Virginia, June 1973-November 1975. Donald H. Rumsfeld, of Illinois. November 1975-January 1977.

ATTORNEY-GENERAL—William B. Saxbe, of Ohio, January 1974-December 1974. Edward H. Levi, of Illinois, January 1975-January 1977.

SECRETARY OF THE INTERIOR—Rogers C.B. Morton, of Maryland, January 1971-March 1975. Stanley K. Hathaway, of Wyoming, June-July 1975. Thomas S. Kleppe, of North Dakota, October 1975-January 1977.

SECRETARY OF AGRICULTURE—Earl L. Butz, of Indiana, December 1971-October 1976.

SECRETARY OF COMMERCE—Frederick B. Dent, of South Carolina, January 1973-March 1975. Rogers C.B. Morton, of Maryland, April 1975-December 1975. Elliot L. Richardson, of Massachusetts, December 1975-January 1977.

SECRETARY OF LABOR—Peter J. Brennan, of New York, February 1973-February 1975. John T. Dunlop, of Maine, March, 1975-January 1976. William J. Usery, Jr., of Georgia, February 1976-January 1977.

SECRETARY OF HEALTH, EDUCATION AND WELFARE—F. David Mathews, of Alabama, August 1975-January 1977.

SECRETARY OF HOUSING AND URBAN DEVELOPMENT—James T. Lynn, of Ohio, February 1973-January 1975. Carla A. Hills, of California, March 1975-January 1977.

SECRETARY OF TRANSPORTATION—William T. Coleman, of Pennsylvania, March 1975-January 1977.

APPENDIX

THE PRESIDENTS AND THE PRESIDENCY:
A Selective Bibliography

THE PRESIDENTS AND THE PRESIDENCY
A Selective Bibliography

Amlund, Curtis A. New perspectives on the Presidency.
New York, Philosophical Library, 1969. 113 p.

Bach, Stanley and George T. Sulzner. Perspectives on
the Presidency; a Collection. Lexington, Mass.,
Heath, 1974. viii, 411 p.

Bagnall, Joseph A. President John F. Kennedy, a Grand
and Global Alliance; the Summons to World Peace
Through World Law. Minneapolis, Burgess Pub. Co.,
1968. xiv, 172 p.

Bailey, Thomas A. Presidential Greatness; the Image and
the Man from George Washington to the Present.
New York, Appleton Century, 1966. xi, 368 p.

Bell, Jack. The Presidency; Office of Power. Boston,
Allyn & Bacon, 1967. v, 182 p.

Binkley, Wilfred E. President and Congress. 3d rev.
ed. New York, Vintage Books, 1962. 403 p.

Brown, Ralph A. The Presidency of John Adams. Lawrence, University Press of Kansas, 1975. x, 248 p.
(American Presidency Series)

Brown, Stuart G. The American Presidency; Leadership,
Partisanship and Popularity. New York, Macmillan,
1966. viii, 279 p.

Brown, Stuart G. The Presidency on Trial; Robert
Kennedy's 1968 Campaign and Afterwards. Honolulu,
University Press of Hawaii, 1972. viii, 155 p.

Brownlow, Louis. The President and the Presidency.
Chicago, Public Administration Service, 1949. 137 p.

Burns, James M. Presidential Government; the Crucible
of Leadership. Boston, Houghton Mifflin, 1973.
xxv, 366 p.

Califano, Joseph. A Presidential Nation. New York,
Norton, 1975. xii, 338 p.

Canfield, Leon H. The Presidency of Woodrow Wilson;
Prelude to a World in Crisis. Rutherford, N. J.,
Fairleigh Dickinson University Press, 1966.
xv, 299 p.

Chamberlain, Lawrence H. The President, Congress and
Legislation. New York, Columbia University Press,
1946. 478 p.

Clark, Keith C. and Laurence J. Legere, eds. The
President and the Management of National Security;
a Report. New York, Praeger, 1969. ix, 274 p.
(Pub. for the Institute for Defense Analysis,
Washington, D. C.)

Coletta, Paolo E. The Presidency of William Howard
Taft. Lawrence, University Press of Kansas, 1973.
ix, 306 p. (American Presidency Series)

Congressional Quarterly, Inc. President Ford: the Man
and His Record. Washington, Congressional Quarterly, Inc., 1974. 79 p.

Cope, Alfred H. and Fred Krinsky, eds. Franklin D.
Roosevelt and the Supreme Court. Rev. ed. Boston,
Heath, 1969. 115 p.

Cornewell, Elmer E. The American Presidency; Vital
Center. Chicago, Scott Foresman, 1966. 166 p.

Corwin, Edward S. The President, Office and Powers,
1787-1957; History and Analysis of Practice and
Opinion. 4th rev. ed. New York, New York
University Press, 1957. 519 p.

Cronin, Thomas E. The State of the Presidency. Boston, Little, Brown, 1975. 355 p.

Cunliffe, Marcus. The American Heritage History of
the Presidency. New York, American Heritage Pub.
Co., 1968. 384 p.

Cunliffe, Marcus. American Presidents and the Presidency. New York, American Heritage Press, 1972.
446 p.

Davison, Kenneth E. The Presidency of Rutherford B.
Hayes. Westport, Ct., Greenwood Press, 1972.
xvii, 266 p. (Contributions in American
Studies)

Dolce, Philip C. and George H. Skau. Power and the
Presidency. New York, Scribner, 1976. xii, 339p.

Earle, Chester B. The President's Powers; Should the
Power of the Presidency be Significantly Curtailed?
Washington, American Enterprise Institute for Public
Policy Research, 1974. iii, 92 p.

Egger, Rowland A. The President of the United States.
    2d ed.   New York, McGraw Hill, 1972.   viii, 198 p.

Falkner, Leonard. The President Who Wouldn't Retire.
    New York, Coward McCann, 1967.   319 p.   (Pres.
    John Quincy Adams)

Farley, James A. Jim Farley's Story; the Roosevelt
    Years.   New York, Whittlesey House, 1948.   388 p.

Feerick, John D. From Failing Hands; the Story of
    Presidential Succession. Foreword by Paul A.
    Freund.   New York, Fordham University Press, 1965.
    xiv, 368 p.

Fisher, Louis. President and Congress; Power and
    Policy.   New York, Free Press, 1972.   xvi, 347 p.

Flatto, Elie. The Second Revolution: Decline and Fall
    of the Presidency.   New York, Arica Press, 1974.
    xi, 93 p.

Hargrove, Erwin C. Presidential Leadership; Personality
    and Political Style.   New York, Macmillan, 1966.
    v, 153 p.

Hargrove, Erwin C. The Power of the Modern Presidency.
    Philadelphia, Temple University Press, 1974.
    xi, 353 p.

Hassler, Warren W. The President as Commander in
    Chief.   Menlo Park, CA., Addison-Wesley Pub. Co.,
    1971.   168 p.

Henry, Laurin L. Presidential Transitions. Washing-
    ton, Brookings Institution, 1960.   xviii, 755 p.

Hersey, John R. The President.   New York, Knopf, 1975.
    xi, 153 p. (First appeared in New York Times
    Magazine April 20, 1975)

Hirschfield, Robert S. The Power of the Presidency;
    Concepts and Controversy.   New York, Atherton,
    1968.   x, 328 p.

Hobbs, Edward H. Behind the President; a Study of
    Executive Office Agencies.   Washington, Public
    Affairs Press, 1954.   248 p.

Hughes, Emmet J. The Living Presidency; the Resources
    and Dilemmas of the American Presidential Office.
    New York, Coward McCann, 1973.   377 p.

James, Dorothy B. _The Contemporary Presidency_. 2d ed.
   Indianapolis, Pegasus, 1974.   xiii, 336 p.

Keogh, James. _President Nixon and the Press_. New
   York, Funk & Wagnalls, 1972.   212 p.

Koenig, Louis W. _The Chief Executive_. 3d ed.
   New York, Harcourt, Brace, Jovanovich, 1975.
   x, 452 p.

Koenig, Louis W. _The Invisible Presidency_. New York,
   Rinehart, 1960.   438 p.

Landecker, Manfred. _The President and Public Opinion;
   Leadership in Foreign Affairs_. Washington, Public
   Affairs Press, 1968.   v, 133 p.

Learned, Henry B. _The President's Cabinet; Studies in
   the Origin, Formation and Structure of an American
   Institution_. New Haven, Yale University Press,
   1912.   471 p.

Lisio, Donal J. _The President and Protest: Hoover,
   Conspiracy and the Bonus Riot_. Columbia, University of Missouri Press, 1974.   viii, 346 p.

McConnell, Grant. _The Modern Presidency_. 2d ed.
   New York, St. Martin's Press, 1976.   133 p.

McDonald, Forrest. _The Presidency of George Washing-
   ton_. Lawrence, University Press of Kansas,
   1974.   xi, 210 p. (American Presidency Series)

Masters, Nicholas A. and Mary E. Baluss. _The Growing
   Powers of the Presidency_. New York, Parent's
   Magazine Press, 1968.   256 p.

May, Ernest R. _The Ultimate Decision; the President
   as Commander in Chief_. New York, Braziller, 1960.
   290 p.

Milton, George F. _The Use of Presidential Power, 1789-
   1943_. Boston, Little, Brown, 1944.   349 p.

Monaghan, Frank. _John Jay, Defender of Liberty against
   Kings & Peoples, Author of the Constitution &
   Governor of New York, President of the Continental
   Congress, Co-author of the Federalist, Negotiator
   of the Peace of 1783 & the Jay Treaty of 1794, First
   Chief Justice of the United States_. Indianapolis,
   Bobbs Merrill, 1935.   497 p.

Mondale, Walter F. _The Accountability of Power; Toward_
a Responsible Presidency. New York, D. McKay,
1975. xix, 284 p.

Montauk Symposium on the Office of the President of
the United States. 2d, 1971. _The Presidency of_
the 1970's; Proceedings. R. Gordon Hoxie, ed.
New York, Center for the Study of the Presidency,
1973. xv, 196 p.

Moos, Malcolm C. _Politics, Presidents, and Coattails_.
Baltimore, Johns Hopkins Press, 1952. xxi, 237 p.

Morgan, Ruth P. _The President and Civil Rights;_
Policy-Making by Executive Order. New York,
St. Martin's Press, 1970. ix, 107 p.

Neustadt, Richard E. _Presidential Power; the Politics_
of Leadership, with Reflections on Johnson and
Nixon. New York, Wiley, 1976. 324 p.

Nikolaieff, George A., comp. _The President and the_
Constitution. New York, H. W. Wilson, 1974.
230 p. (Reference Shelf v. 46, no. 4)

Nunnerley, David. _President Kennedy and Britain_.
New York, St. Martin's Press, 1972. xii, 242 p.

Parton, James. _The Presidency of Andrew Jackson_.
Ed. with an Introd. and Notes by Robert V. Remini.
New York, Harper & Row, 1967. xxxvii, 468 p.

Patterson, Caleb P. _Presidential Government in the_
United States; the Unwritten Constitution. Chapel
Hill, University of North Carolina Press, 1947.
301 p.

Pritchett, Charles H. _The Roosevelt Court; a Study in_
Judicial Politics and Values, 1937-1947. New
York, Macmillan, 1948. xvi, 314 p.

Reedy, George E., advisory ed. _The Presidency_. New
York, New York Times, 1975. xi, 468 p. Articles
from the New York Times.

Reedy, George E. _The Presidency in Flux_. New York,
Columbia University Press, 1973. vii, 133 p.

Reedy, George E. _The Twilight of the Presidency_.
New York, New American Library, 1971. xv, 191 p.

Rose, Richard. Managing Presidential Objectives.
New York, Free Press, 1976.   x, 180 p.

Rossiter, Clinton L. The American Presidency. With a
new introd. by D. W. Brogan.   New York, Time, Inc.,
1963.   xxi, 319 p.

Russell, Francis. The President Makers: from Mark
Hanna to Joseph P. Kennedy.   Boston, Little,
Brown, 1976.   vi, 407 p.

Schouler, James. History of the United States of
America, under the Constitution.   New York, Dodd,
Mead, 1894-1913.   7 v.   Contents: v. 1. 1783-1801.
Rule of federalism.--v. 2. 1801-1817. Jefferson
Republicans.--v. 3. 1817-1831. Era of good feeling.
--v. 4. 1831-1847. Democrats and Whigs.--v. 5.
1847-1861. Free soil controversy.--v. 6. 1861-1865.
The Civil War.--v. 7. 1876-1877. The Reconstruction
period.

Smith, A. Merriman. A President is Many Men.   New
York, Harper, 1948.   269 p.

Smith, Elbert B. The Presidency of James Buchanan.
Lawrence, University Press of Kansas, 1975.
xiii, 225 p. (American Presidency Series)

Smith, John M. and Stephen Jurika, Jr. The President
and National Security; His Role as Commander-in-
Chief.   Dubuque, Ia., Kendall/Hunt Pub. Co., 1972.
xvi, 303 p.

Stanwood, Edward. A History of the Presidency.   New
ed., rev. by Charles Knowles Bolton.   Boston,
Houghton Mifflin (193-?)   2 v.

Strum, Philippa. Presidential Power and American
Democracy.   Pacific Palisades, CA., Goodyear, 1972.
xi, 132 p.

Stryker, Lloyd P. Andrew Johnson, a Study in Courage.
New York, Macmillan, 1930.   xvi, 881 p.

Thomas, Norman C. The Presidency in Contemporary
Context.   New York, Dodd, Mead, 1975.   viii, 348p.

Tugwell, Rexford G. and Thomas E. Cronin. The Presidency Reappraised.   New York, Praeger, 1974.
vi, 312 p.

United States. Congress. Senate. Committee on the
    Judiciary. Subcommittee on Constitutional Amend-
    ments. Election of the President. Hearings, 89th
    Congress Second Session and 90th Congress First
    Session. Washington, U. S. Govt. Print. Off.,
    1968. v, 948 p.

Vinyard, Dale. The Presidency. New York, Scribner,
    1971. x, 214 p.

Wann, A. J. The President as Chief Administrator; a
    Study of Franklin D. Roosevelt. Washington,
    Public Affairs Press, 1968. v, 219 p.

Warren, Sidney. The President as World Leader.
    New York, McGraw Hill, 1967. xii, 480 p.

White, Leonard D. The Jacksonians, 1829-1861. New
    York, Macmillan, 1954. 593 p.

White, Leonard D. The Republican era, 1869-1901.
    New York, Macmillan, 1958. 406 p.

Wildavsky, Aaron B., ed. The Presidency. Boston,
    Little, Brown, 1969. xv, 795 p.

Winston, Robert W. Andrew Johnson, Plebeian and
    Patriot. New York, Holt, 1928. xvi, 549 p.

Wise, Sidney and Richard Schier. The Presidential
    Office. New York, Crowell, 1968. vii, 248 p.

Wolk, Allan. The Presidency and Black Civil Rights:
    Eisenhower to Nixon. Rutherford, N. J., Fairleigh
    Dickinson University Press, 1971. 276 p.